Fun Afloat

Cool Activities for Families that Boat

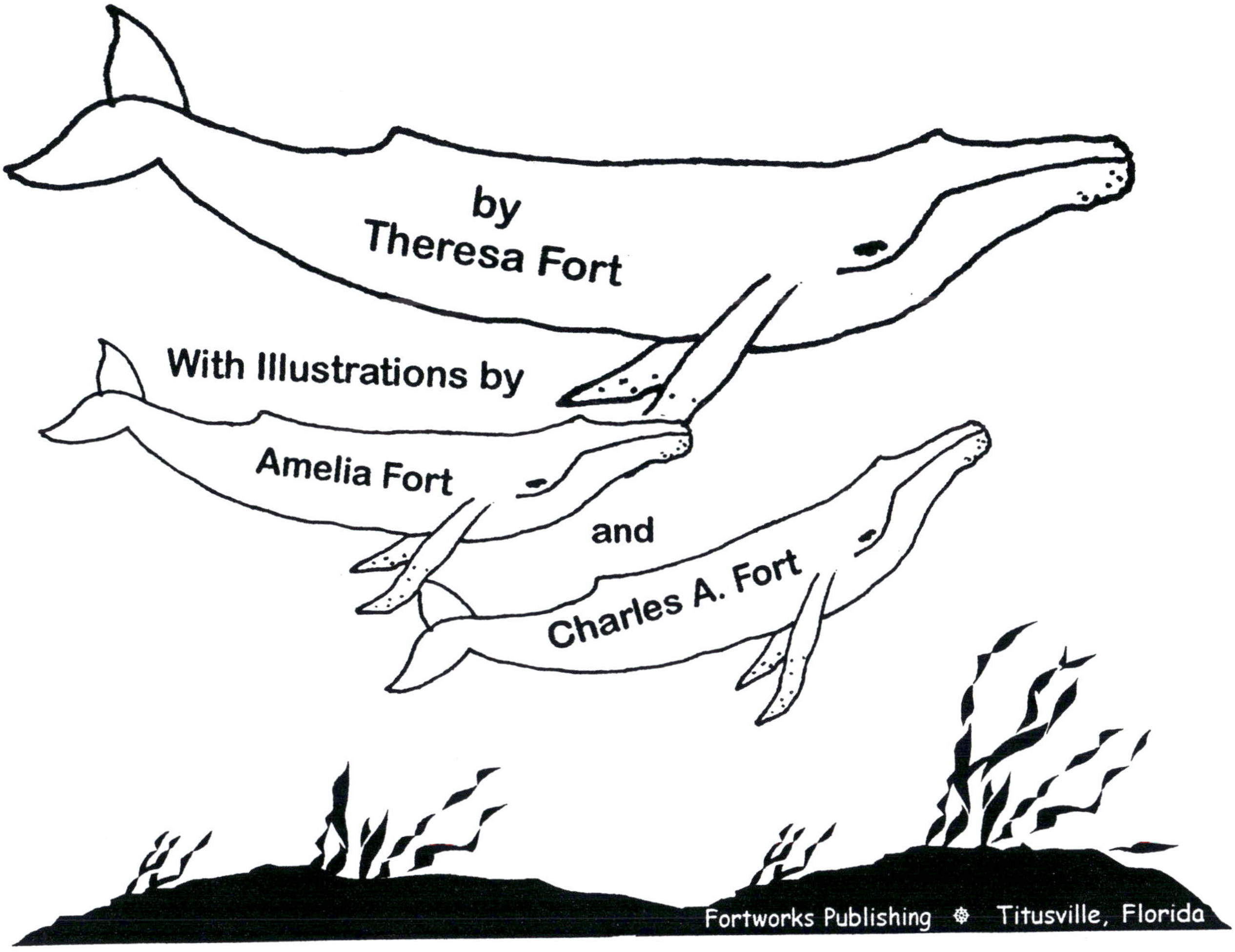

To Amie and Alex

Fun Afloat!
Cool Activities for Families that Boat

Cover Design: Charles D. Fort
Illustrations: Theresa Fort
Amelia Fort
Charles A. Fort

Published by
Fortworks Publishing
Post Office Box 6766
Titusville, FL 32782-6766
publishing@fortworks.com
http://publishing.fortworks.com

Printed in the United States of America

1st Edition

Library of Congress Card Number: 00-193007

ISBN 0-9706289-0-0

Notice to Mariners

Setting Sail

Fun Afloat began as a group of ideas and activities I gathered to help make boating more fun and possibly more educational for our two children as we introduced them to boating, and later as we began cruising abroad. It grew as I modified activities I found in books, or as I talked to other boating families. Our family and friends have had fun testing these activities. I hope that you find them as enjoyable as we have!

I invite you to explore the book thoroughly. Many of the activities have tables and forms to use that are found in the back of the book. You will find several choices of forms and tables for each so that you can pick the best for your situation. Some are blank so that you can create your own. Or, buy our inexpensive comb bound journals with the order form on page 171.

If you boat part time, some of the activities can be done at home, and the items made can be taken with you to use while you are boating.

Disclaimer

Every possible effort has been made to test each activity for its appropriateness aboard a boat and to assure that each is easy to understand and accomplish. Differences in supplies used can result in differences in outcomes.

This activity book is intended to be used as a family. It is assumed that parents will actively supervise or be a part of the activities. Some activities involve the use of sharp objects and varying depths of water. It is up to each parent or guardian to decide the appropriateness of each activity for every child involved.

Vessel Layout

The Chart Table is your Table of Contents, the place that will give you direction and course headings for activities and other areas aboard.

The Activity Area is where all activities are stowed.

The Cargo Hold is your resource area.

Compartment A contains all the forms and tables you may need for the activities. At the end, you will find graph paper and lined paper for your own use.

Compartment B holds identification guides and extra information that may be helpful to you concerning whales and dolphins, weather, seaweed, as well as plankton and other tiny life.

The Bilge is the place to go to look up an activity by the topic. It also contains a bibliography and reference guide for other places to go for marine related information. Like the bilge on a real boat, it is often the last place to look for the treasure you are seeking, and the typical place to find it. Our little stowaway, Earl, hides in its darkest corners.

Explanation of Navigation Symbols

The lighthouse will give you ideas to help get the most from an activity.

Ahoy! I'm Captain J. Peg. I'll provide you with interesting information.

The life ring has helpful information or timesaving advice.

Need help finding an activity? Just ask me, Earl. I'm a stow away here. I know where all the treasures are kept. Find me hiding in the bilge.

Crew List

Like a captain without a good crew, this book would have failed to set sail without all the people that helped in even the smallest way. Thank-you to:

Debbie Lyons and **Margrit Gahlinger** for their tireless work editing and proof-reading plus their addition of wonderful ideas during the beginning stages of this book.

Nigel and Terry Calder for their expert advice, particularly in the beginning stages.

Deb Linder for supporting me when my course of action disappeared.

Trevor Spradlin of the NOAA, National Marine Fisheries Service, Office of Protected Resources, for guidelines on whale watching.

Dagmar Fertl, marine mammal biologist, for professional guidance about whale identification and whale behavior.

All cruisers that we came into contact with during our travel. It is through you that I was inspired.

But, most of all, THANK-YOU **Chuck, Amie, and Alex** for putting up with my typing at all hours of the day and night, late meals for many months , a pre-occupied mom and wife that didn't always listen when she needed to, and for the help you gave to this project!

Chuck, you are a masterful detail person. Thank-you for all of the hours you put into editing and proofreading the final draft!

Amie, thank you for the effort you put into your illustrations and your patience in teaching me to draw.

Alex, you are wonderful at coming up with fun project ideas and testing them.

I couldn't have asked for a better crew! Thank-you all!

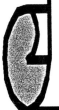

Don't GO through life,
grow through life!

Chart Table

Looks like fun's a brewin' Mates!

Cargo Manifest

Here are some general items to bring aboard for fun. For specific supplies needed, check individual activities.

- ☒ *Paper—both lined and unlined*
- ☒ *Graph paper*
- ☒ *Colored construction paper*
- ☒ *Erasers*
- ☒ *Ruler*
- ☒ *Stapler*
- ☒ *Scissors*
- ☒ *Glue*
- ☒ *Pencils and pencil sharpener*
- ☒ *Markers, water-based for easy wash up as well as waterproof*
- ☒ *Field guides to animals, plants, shells, minerals, clouds*
- ☒ *Books on ocean animals, particularly whales*
- ☒ *Charts of all areas through which you will be traveling*
- ☒ *Charting tools such as dividers, plotters, rulers*
- ☒ *Clock or watch*
- ☒ *Good quality magnifying glass*
- ☒ *Leftover boxes, old magazines, glitter, scraps of fabric, trim, etc.*
- ☒ *A small globe*
- ☒ *Small musical instruments: harmonica, mouth harp, recorder, etc.*
- ☒ *Deck of cards*
- ☒ *Reference books on subjects of interest*
- ☒ *Folders for making journals*

Photo Journal

 Make a photo journal of a special boating adventure, a visit to a country, or tailor it to your interests. It's a great idea for trips to historic sites, national parks, or cities.

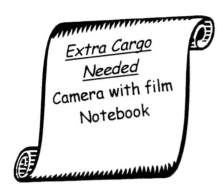

Extra Cargo Needed
Camera with film
Notebook

Getting Underway

Pick a topic for your photo journal. Think about what kind of pictures would best illustrate the idea before beginning.

Be particular about the photos but also take chances and try new ideas. Keep track of the photos by writing down what is included in each picture taken.

When the photos are developed, put them into a small notebook and write an explanation for each picture. Fun, creativity, and imagination should rule.

Topic Ideas

📖 Document animals and plants you spot from the boat.

📖 Record types of boats you see.

📖 Create a photo journal of a whole boat trip. Take pictures of every activity until coming back to your home.

📖 Make a photo journal of what it's like to live aboard a boat. Include pictures that illustrate everyday chores and activities as well as pictures of some of the excitement.

📖 Create a photo journal of each anchorage or port you visit.

Disposable cameras can be bought and kept just for this activity!

Alternate Courses

- If you make a journal about living aboard a boat, send it to family or friends so that they can understand what it's like to live aboard.
- Write a fictional story, then take photos to illustrate it. You could make up a story about some of your toys then photograph them in poses that tell your story.

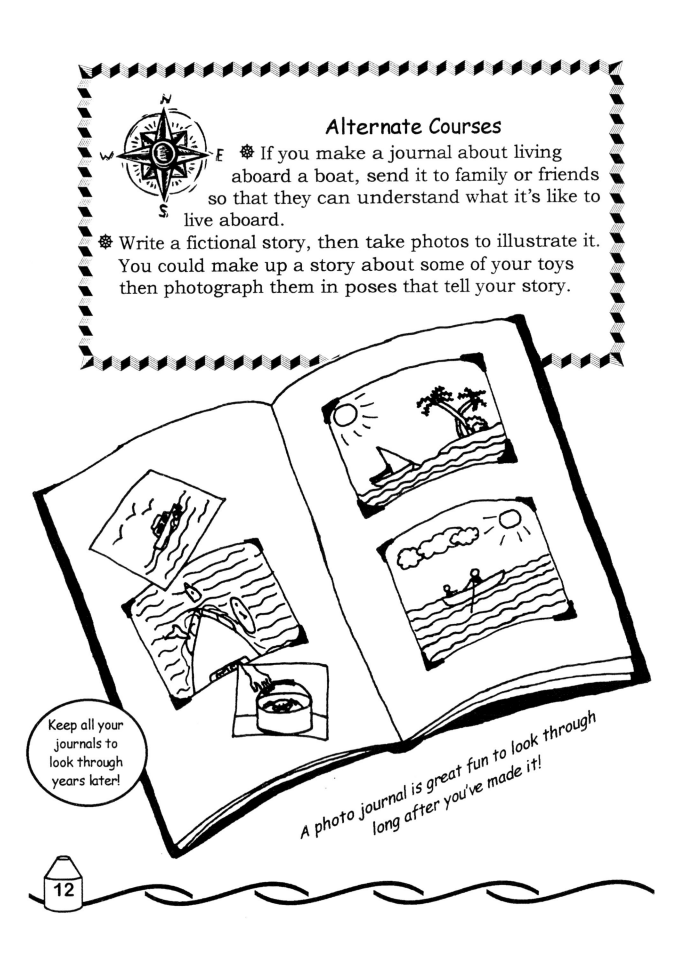

Keep all your journals to look through years later!

A photo journal is great fun to look through long after you've made it!

Map your Trip

Keep track of your route on a map as you travel. It is a fun way to hone your geography and map reading skills. In this activity the word "map" is used to suggest something other than navigational charts.

Extra Cargo
Needed
Map
Highlighter pen or
fine line marker

Our Trip

Getting Underway

As you travel, have a general map of the area hung up on a bulkhead to record your voyage. Mark distances and directions traveled during day hops and passages.

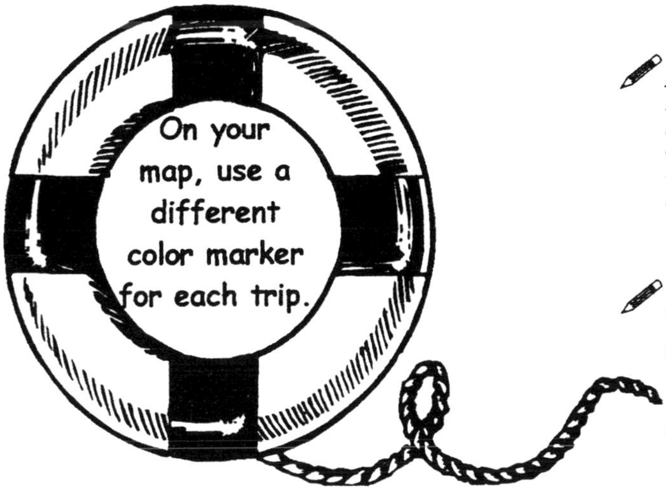
On your
map, use a
different
color marker
for each trip.

Ideas

- As you sight a landmark shown on your map, highlight it, then write in the time and the weather.
- Mark places where you saw a special animal, where you anchored for lunch, or stopped to fish.

Including its islands, Alaska has over 30,000 miles of coastline!

The first maps were made on clay tablets in Babylonia around 2300 B.C.

Alternate Courses

- Draw a map of the area where you are boating. Then mark your course. Include fishing stops, animals seen, or even a picture of your boat with family aboard.
- If you boat short distances from a home port, mark the routes used and places explored along with the dates of the outings.
- If you are on a long trip, keep track of your entire trip by having a large area map or even a world map always up on a bulkhead. Mark your daily or weekly progress.
- Where would you go if you were planning a trip of your own? Design your own route on a map and pick special places to stop and explore.
- Keep a small globe on board to find where new friends are from.

Russia has the longest continuous coastline of any country. It stretches 23,400 miles!

Magellan's crew were the first Europeans to circumnavigate the Earth.

Flag Journal

Keep a flag journal of the different national flags you see as you travel on your boat. It will give you a sense of belonging to a world economy. This is especially fun if you happen to live or boat near a major port.

Extra Cargo Needed

Three ring binder or folder
Hole punch
Flag identification guide

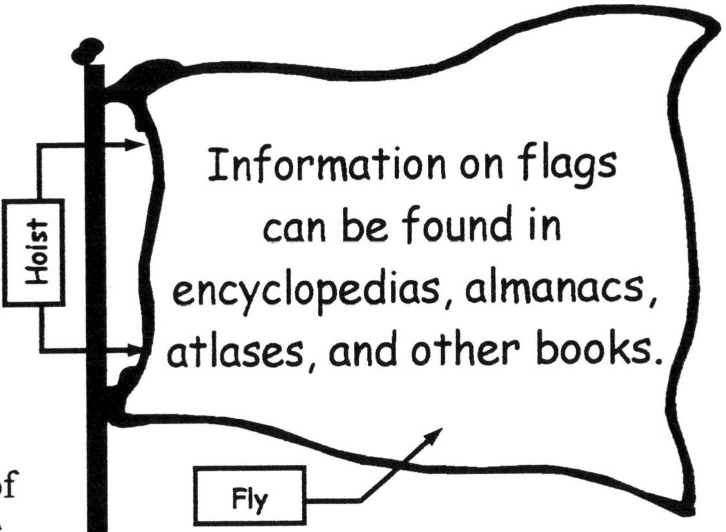

Hoist
Information on flags can be found in encyclopedias, almanacs, atlases, and other books.
Fly

Getting Underway

Record the nationalities of the ships and boats you see as you travel. In your folder, use colored pencils or markers to draw the different flags you see. Identify them.

Include the information below:

- Time and location of the vessel
- Type of vessel
- Direction the vessel was heading

In your journal, use one full page per country so that you can include other sightings for the same country. Arrange the pages alphabetically so that you can find countries easier. As you identify more and more flags, you'll be forming your own flag identification guide.

Ideas

- Make an educated guess as to what each ship is carrying as cargo.
- Standing ship-watch when near shipping lanes is a good way to see new flags and help keep your boat safe at the same time.

Look in Compartment A of the Cargo Hold for Flag Journal pages you can photocopy and use. Or, see page 171 to order our inexpensive comb bound journals.

The first flags were probably feathers flown from long sticks used to identify different tribes of people.

Alternate Courses

- With an adult, call the ships you see using your VHF. Try to start up a conversation if the radio operator seems cordial. Ask if they can see you on radar. Find out where they are headed. They are capable of giving you a great deal of important information such as your position, speed, and heading from their radar as well as excellent weather forecasts.
- Discount retailers often have inexpensive world flag posters that you can use to circle flags seen as you travel.
- Make up a story about a ship. Invent what their cargo is, who is on board, where it is going, even adventures it has already had. What will happen to them next?
- Some world maps have flag identification information along their border. You can keep track of flag sightings, then mark the country on the map.

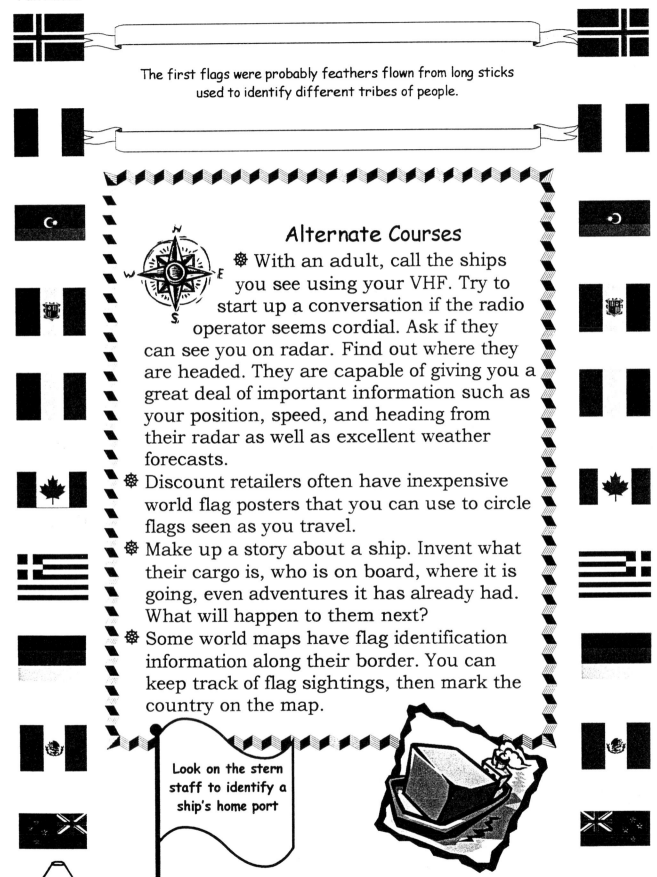

Look on the stern staff to identify a ship's home port

Calculate your Travel Time

Learn how to calculate your travel times for a passage, distances you'll be traveling, and estimated times of arrival to a port or anchorage. Then you won't have to ask anyone, "Are we there yet?"

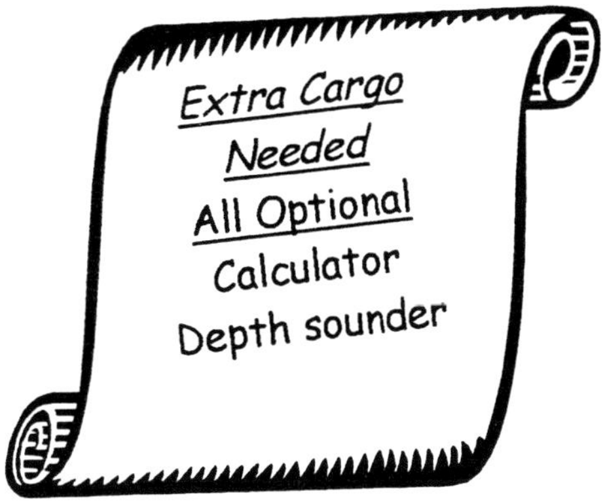

Getting Underway

Lay out the chart of your area on a flat surface. Find obvious physical coastal features, any buoys or other navigational aids, and your depth that correlates to features and depth readings you have experienced along the way. Then use additional information from your dead reckoning, course heading for the day, and any past fixes to confirm your location.

If you happen to have a GPS, you can use it to confirm your position. Then plot your position on your chart using the latitude and longitude. You have found where you are. Next, find your destination on the chart. Now you will need to figure the distance to your destination.

Finding Distances

To figure out how many nautical miles there are to your destination, use your dividers. Position them along the scale on the part of your chart that shows the length of a nautical mile and size them to this area.

Then "walk" the dividers from where you are now to your destination, following your approximate route, and counting the miles as you go.

This symbol can save you time!

Finding Your ETA

ETA is short for estimated time of arrival. To find out when you will you be at your destination you will need to use the formula below:

It's easy to use the handy symbol above.
D= Distance, S= Speed, and T= Time. Just cover up the variable you are looking for to find the operation needed.

Examples:

A. *If you need to find Time, putting your finger over the T will show you to divide Distance by Speed.*
B. *If you need Distance, putting your finger over D, will show you to multiply Speed by Time.*

Time = Distance ÷ Speed

(Or see the life ring for a handy trick)

Divide your distance in nautical miles by your speed in knots, and that's how many hours you have to travel. Add those hours to the time on your watch and that's the general time you will arrive if you continue to travel at your current speed.

Alternate Courses

☸Learn how the depth sounder and GPS are read and used. Learn the proper way to turn both on, get readings, and use the information.

☸Get involved with the chart work as you travel. Dead reckoning and plotting positions from the GPS are abilities that will help hone your math skills as well as help you operate the boat someday.

Currents

The calculations from this activity do not take into account any currents. If you are boating in an area where there are measurable currents, you will need to factor that into your calculations.

Tidal Currents are the horizontal movement of water due to the rise and fall of tidal levels.
Flood- a tidal current that flows from the sea to the shore.
Ebb- a tidal current that flows from the shore out to sea.

Ocean currents come from relatively constant winds.

Currents Directly Against You

Currents directly against you decrease your speed over ground by the same amount as their speed. To figure out your speed with an adverse current, subtract the current's speed from your speed through the water. If you are traveling 5 knots through the water with a 2 knot current against you, your actual speed over ground will be 3 knots.

Currents Directly with You

Currents directly with you increase your speed over ground. To figure your speed with a favorable current, simply add your speed through the water to the current's speed. If you are traveling 6 knots with a favorable current with you of 3 knots, your speed over ground will be 9 knots.

The **drift** of a current is its speed.

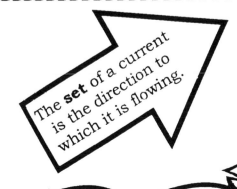

The **set** of a current is the direction to which it is flowing.

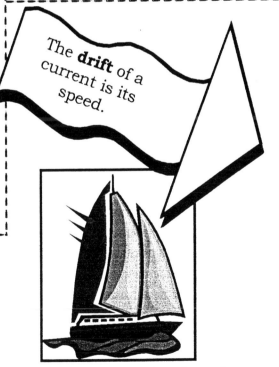

Ah! Current and wind with you!

Does it Float?

Water is always fun to play with and in this activity you can experiment with little items around the boat to see if they float and carry cargo.

Extra Cargo Needed

Miscellaneous items from the boat
Large bucket or basin
Surrounding water

Getting Underway

Fill your bucket or basin with your surrounding water. Then experiment with different objects to see which float and which do not. Now, using available materials, design and make different shaped boats. Which shape works best for buoyancy?

Add marbles or other small objects one at a time into the boat. What happens when you load your model boat? What happens when the load is unbalanced? Balanced?

Ideas

- Experiment with all sorts of caps, bottle tops, and shallow cans as boat hulls. Which shapes hold the most cargo?
- Try floating a small sheet of aluminum foil. Will it hold any cargo? Then form it so that it has sides and more of a hull shape. Can it carry more or less cargo? Will it float balled up?
- In an empty basin add different sizes and shapes of wood. Slowly add water and see which floats first. Before you start to add any water, try to guess which will be the first to float and how much water will be needed.

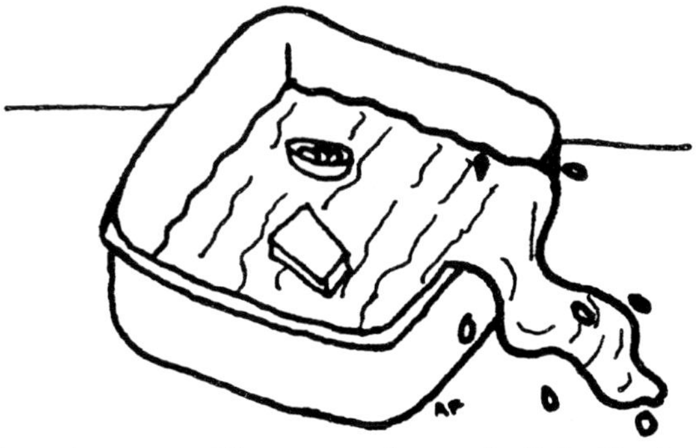

Just in case spills occur, the cockpit is the best place to do your experimenting!

Find your Speed Through the Water

It's fun to figure out how fast your boat is going by using mathematics and a little biodegradable debris.

Extra Cargo Needed
Watch with second hand
Vegetable debris
Calculator

WARNING:
This activity is not intended for speeds greater than 10 knots. When traveling at faster speeds, see page 25 for another way to measure your speed.

WATCH OUT!

Before doing this activity, check regulations regarding overboard discharge.

Getting Underway

At least two people are required for this activity. Position one at the bow with the vegetable matter and one at the stern with the watch. The person safely perched at the bow of your boat drops a piece of fruit or vegetable right to the side of the boat's bow and in front, then signals to the timekeeper at the stern to begin timing. The person at the stern then measures how long the piece takes to reach the very end of the boat and records the number of seconds on paper.

Now use this amount of time along with the length of your boat to find your speed through the water.

Step 1: Speed = Distance ÷ Time

If you know any two of the above terms, you can figure out the third. This time we know distance and time. But, we need to know distance in terms of nautical miles and time in terms of hours to figure out your speed in knots (nautical miles per hour).

Remember This? *(See page 18)*

Step 2: Converting Feet to Nautical Miles

First take the length of your boat in feet and divide it by 6,000 which is roughly the number of feet in a nautical mile (To be exact use 6,076 feet).

Length of boat in feet ÷ 6,000 = Distance your boat traveled in nautical miles. *(continued)*

Step 3: Converting Seconds to Hours

Now you'll need to convert the number of seconds the debris traveled into hours. Do this by dividing your time in seconds by 3,600, which is the number of seconds in one hour.

The seconds your debris traveled the length of boat ÷ 3,600 = Time in hours your debris traveled.

You can make your own log line on page 25.

Ahoy mates! Sailors began referring to their speed in knots because they used to throw a knotted length of line overboard with a log attached. They would time themselves for six seconds and count the knots that were released during those seconds. The number of knots was their speed!

Step 4: Final Calculations

Now comes the time to use our important formula, S = D ÷ T

Your boat's speed in knots = Distance in nautical miles your boat moved ÷ Time elapsed in hours.

An example:

On a 40 foot boat, Nina counts 9 seconds for an orange peel to travel the length of her boat from stem to stern. How fast is her boat traveling?

40 ft. boat ÷ 6000 = 0.00667 nm

6 seconds ÷ 3600 = 0.00167 hours

0.00667 ÷ 0.00167 = ***4.01 knots***

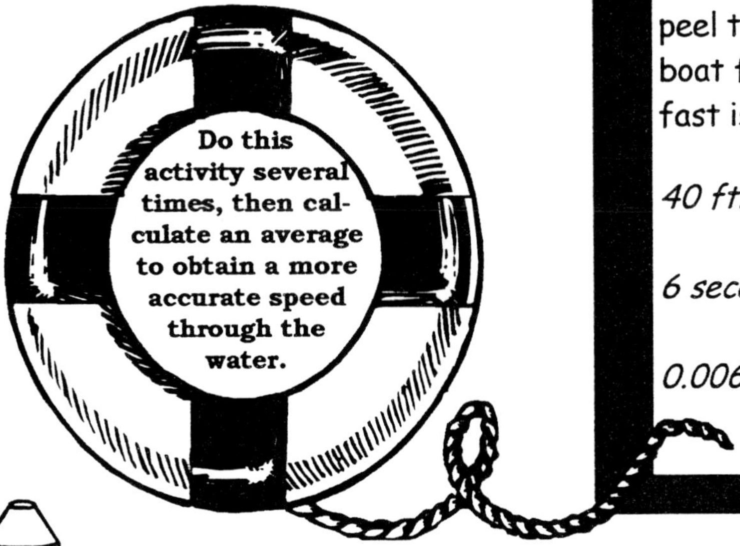

Do this activity several times, then calculate an average to obtain a more accurate speed through the water.

Keep Track of Boating Distances

Record daily distances for each of your short trips or for a long voyage. Either way, you'll be surprised at how the miles add up!

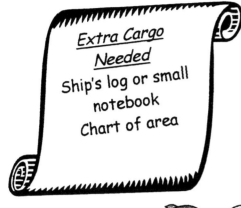

Extra Cargo Needed

Ship's log or small notebook

Chart of area

Getting Underway

Step 1:

By using your dividers and a chart showing your beginning and ending positions, you can calculate your distance for the last 24 hours. Adjust your dividers to the scale on the chart to measure nautical miles and walk the dividers from the beginning to the ending position on the chart.

Distance = Speed × Time

You can also calculate an estimate of the distance traveled by using your day's average speed and your travel time. If your boating area has a measurable current, you may need to factor for it. See page 19 for information on currents.

Step 2:

Log the day's distance in your ship's log. If you don't have a log, you can photocopy one of the logs from Compartment A of the Cargo Hold, or order a customized Ship's Log with the order form on page 171.

Ideas

1. Calculate how far your family goes each month or year.
2. Keep track of your average distance traveled daily, monthly, and even yearly.
3. Track your total distance traveled during a particular part of a trip or even a whole trip.

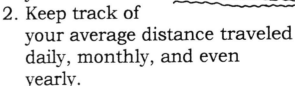

Story Building

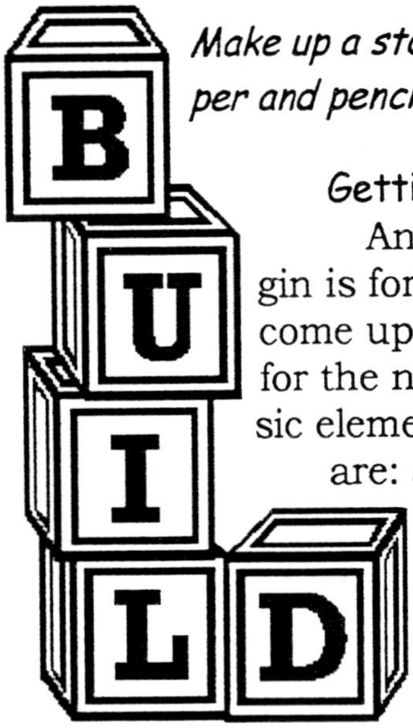

Make up a story together as you travel aboard your boat. All you need is paper and pencil or a cassette recorder and cassette tape.

Getting Underway

An easy way to begin is for each person to come up with an element for the new story. The basic elements of a story are: a setting (time and place), a character or two, and a problem or challenge. With each element decided upon, the group decides who will be first. That person then comes up with a beginning and the other players add to it.

Be as descriptive as possible with each addition to the story. You can take turns or brainstorm together. If conditions are rough, tape your story on a tape recorder and add sound effects along the way. If the weather is calm write the story down.

It is fun to watch the changes your stories go through as you get more practice in building them. The stories begin to have more depth and detail with time.

Having a separate journal for these stories is an interesting way to see how your stories develop over time. Draw pictures of your characters and maps of their adventures and homes.

Alternate Courses

- Build a continuing story whenever you are aboard your boat. Made up characters could have different adventures every time you are aboard.

- You could make up a whole world or your own island with characters that change. Let your imaginations run wild. Be creative and descriptive with your ideas.

Counting Knots

Find your speed the old fashioned way with a log line by counting knots in the line as it streams over the stern.

In most cases you will need at least 85 feet of line to measure the speed of a boat that can go up to 6 knots.

Extra Cargo Needed

Plastic milk jug, partially filled with water
50-100 feet of light weight line
Colorful strip of cloth

Getting Underway

Tie one end of the light weight line securely to your partially filled plastic milk jug.

Measure 20 feet from the jug along the line and tie the cloth strip to the line. Then tie the line to the cloth strip knot so it will not slip.

Now, make a knot in the line every ten feet. Your log line is done!

At faster speeds, use a much longer line and stream out the line for twelve seconds. Divide the number of knots by two to get your speed.

Using your Log Line

Attach the free end to a stern cleat so that you will not accidentally release all your line overboard. Feed all the line underneath any stern rails that might get in the way. And, make sure there are no kinks in the line, or that there is nothing to get in the way as the line is released. You will want it to flow freely from your hands. *(continued)*

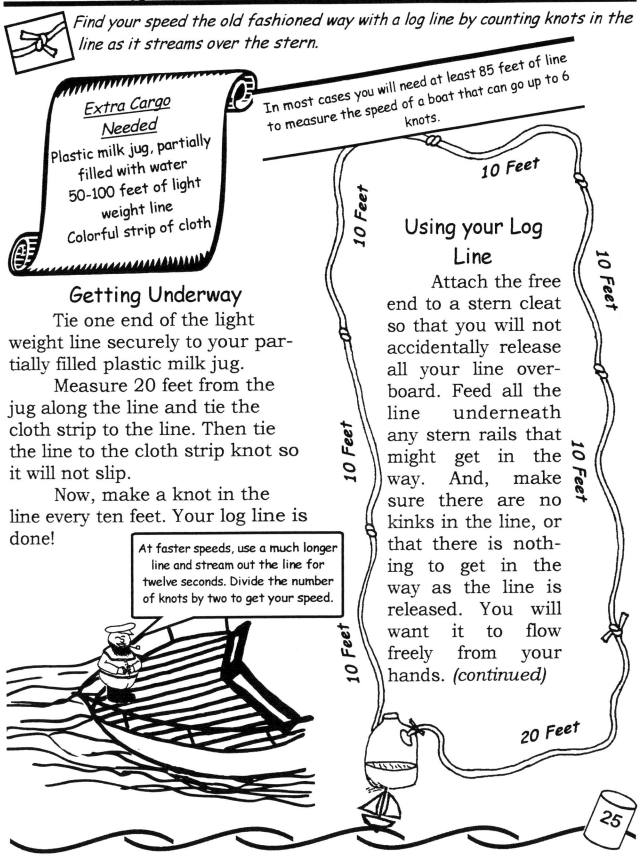

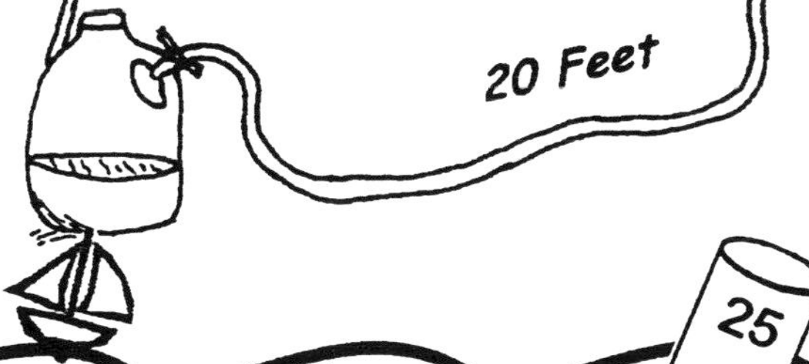

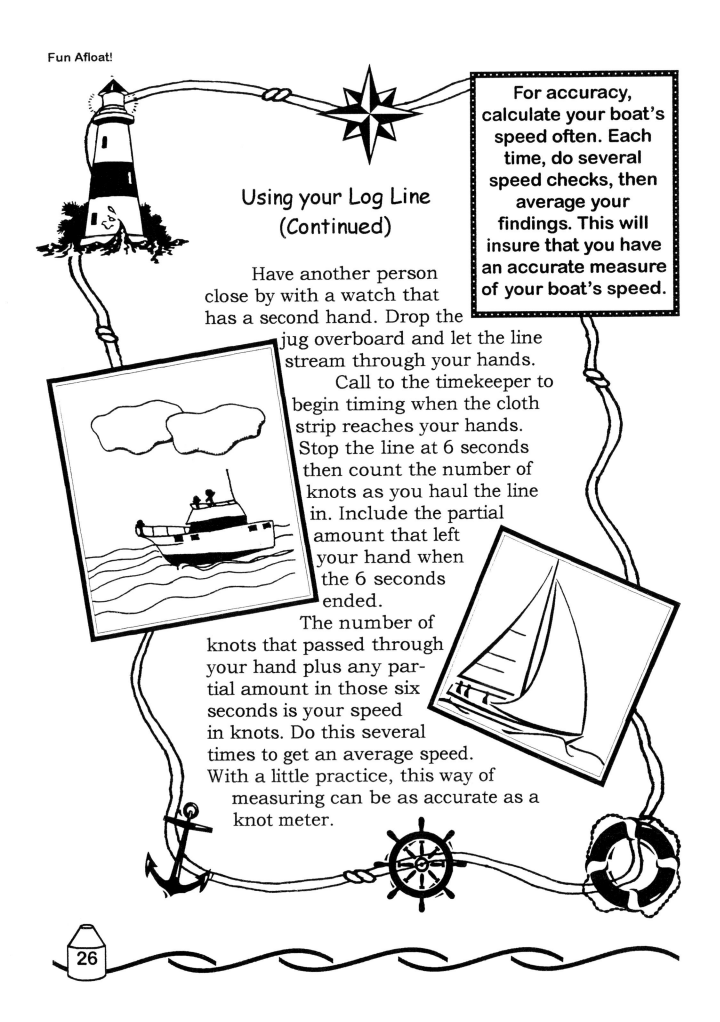

For accuracy, calculate your boat's speed often. Each time, do several speed checks, then average your findings. This will insure that you have an accurate measure of your boat's speed.

Using your Log Line (Continued)

Have another person close by with a watch that has a second hand. Drop the jug overboard and let the line stream through your hands.

Call to the timekeeper to begin timing when the cloth strip reaches your hands. Stop the line at 6 seconds then count the number of knots as you haul the line in. Include the partial amount that left your hand when the 6 seconds ended.

The number of knots that passed through your hand plus any partial amount in those six seconds is your speed in knots. Do this several times to get an average speed. With a little practice, this way of measuring can be as accurate as a knot meter.

Sound Journal

Keeping a sound journal is a fun activity with the help of a portable tape recorder. You can record sounds of animals encountered, the din of a big city anchorage, or even the noises of life underway as you motor or sail.

Make the hydrophone on page 109 and use it for your sound journal.

Extra Cargo Needed

Portable tape recorder
Blank tapes

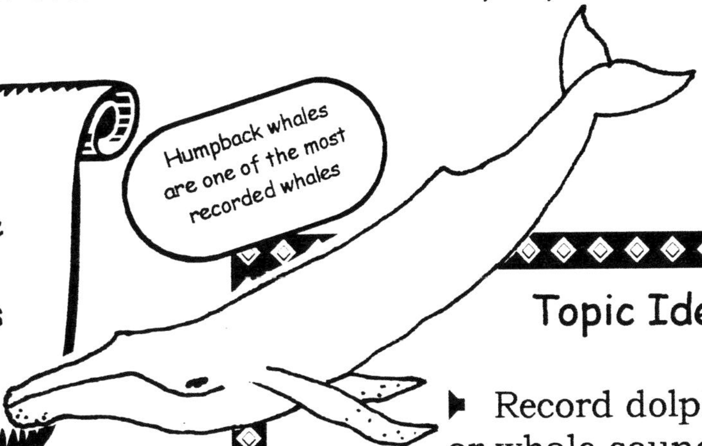

Humpback whales are one of the most recorded whales

Getting Underway

1. Pick a topic and think about what kinds of sounds will best illustrate it.

2. Think about the following questions before you begin: Will there be a narrator? Do you want to interview someone involved with the topic? If so, what kind of questions should be asked?

3. For better organization, make an outline of the ideas and sounds you want to capture. Or, choose to have a freeform tape and tape whatever comes to mind.

4. Set aside one tape for each topic idea you want to try.

5. Remember, mistakes can be erased and recorded over.

Topic Ideas

- Record dolphin or whale sounds if you are lucky enough to have them come close.
- Tape a day-to-day journal of your adventures aboard.
- Document noises of each anchorage or marina.
- Record life aboard your boat.
- Act as a reporter or narrator during the tape.
- Interview the captain and crew.

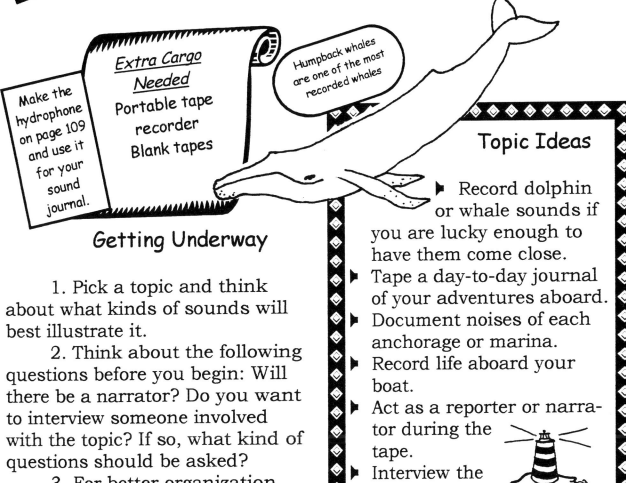

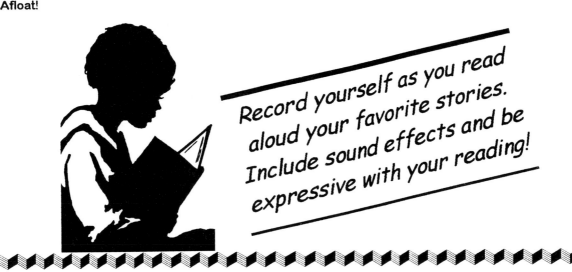

Record yourself as you read aloud your favorite stories. Include sound effects and be expressive with your reading!

Alternate Courses

- Record the activities of a day trip.
- Make a tape of family life aboard your boat to send to friends or extended family at home. It is a wonderful chance for people at home to experience a part of your trip.
- If you do schoolwork aboard your boat, tape a full day of school. Try to forget the recorder is on and go about your business. Then play the tape, listening carefully. Brainstorm ideas for making school time an even better experience.
- Record yourself reading favorite short stories. Have fun by including sound effects or music in the background.

Secret Spot

Secretly pick a place on your chart and answer questions to reveal its identity. This is a version of the 20 question game most of us are familiar with, tailored to boating.

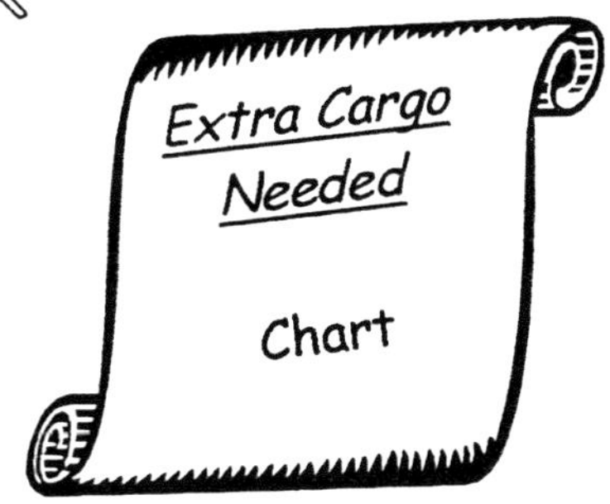

Getting Underway

The number of players is up to you for this 20-question game, but each player needs to be able to see and read the chart. Younger players can get help from the older ones by playing in teams. Alone, one person/team picks a secret spot on the chart you are using. Then, other players take turns asking questions to guess the spot chosen. Ask questions so that you can eliminate large areas on the chart. The one who guesses correctly is the next one to pick a secret spot.

Ideas

- ⊗ Picking places you have visited is a good idea for younger players because the questions and answers can be more detailed.
- ⊗ When picking a new place you've never been to, pick one that has a lot of detail to it on the chart.
- ⊗ Decide if your questions will only be answered with a yes or no, or will have more detailed answers.
- ⊗ When asking questions, study the chart and ask about features and navigation aids close by.
- ⊗ Study the area of the chart you choose before letting anyone know you are ready for their questions.

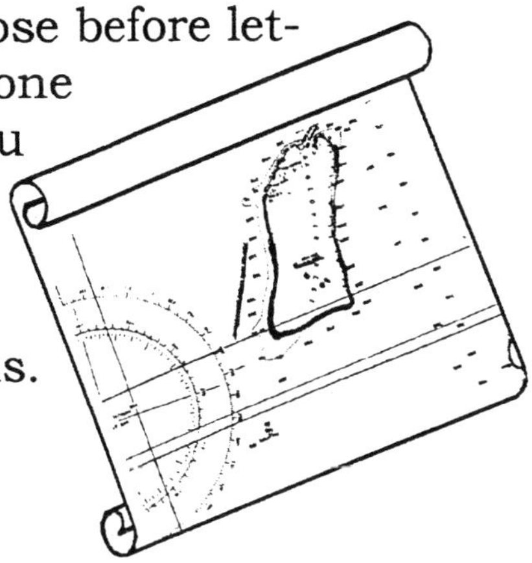

Design your Own Postcards

Tired of buying postcards? Looking for a postcard that is unique? Try designing and sending your own postcards.

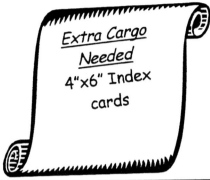

Extra Cargo Needed

4"x6" Index cards

Getting Underway

Draw pictures of your adventures on one side of an index card. Use waterproof markers and put in as much detail as possible so that the receiver can live your adventure through your eyes.

Then use the other side for a short letter. Draw a vertical line on the writing side to separate where the address and stamp will go.

Alternate Courses

- When you process film of your boating adventures, choose to have them made into the 4"x6" size. Then you can glue them to your 4"x6" index cards to make photo postcards.
- If you get attached to any of your designer postcards, mail them to yourself as souvenirs.

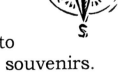

Daily Journal

A daily journal is an excellent way to learn how to express feelings and keep track of your trip, and is a wonderful souvenir to keep.

Extra Cargo Needed

Notebook or blank journal

See Compartment A of the Cargo Hold for a reproducible Daily Journal page.

Getting Underway

Set up a nighttime ritual of writing in your journal before bed as a way to unwind from the day. Expressing yourself on paper has a way of releasing daily pressures and challenges that could otherwise build up inside. If you spend weekends aboard your boat, keep a journal aboard to write about your boating adventures.

Record your feelings and experiences about the places you travel. Include as much information as possible about the conditions that you find and the adventures that you have. It may be interesting to share your writing with other boaters going to the same areas you visited. And, it will be great to read it for yourself if you return to those same places.

If you have trouble deciding what to write about, ask yourself, "How did I feel today?" Then concentrate your writing on those feelings. You'll find that when you look back through your journal, you will enjoy the entries that include your feelings more than the ones that explain only about where you traveled.

Alternate Courses

- Try a talking journal. Tape the story of your day on a cassette recorder and create a memorable journal. Sound effects and interviews of friends can be added as well.
- Make a trip calendar. Buy or draw a calendar with large squares for each day so that you can draw a picture or write a few words about happenings for each day of your trip.

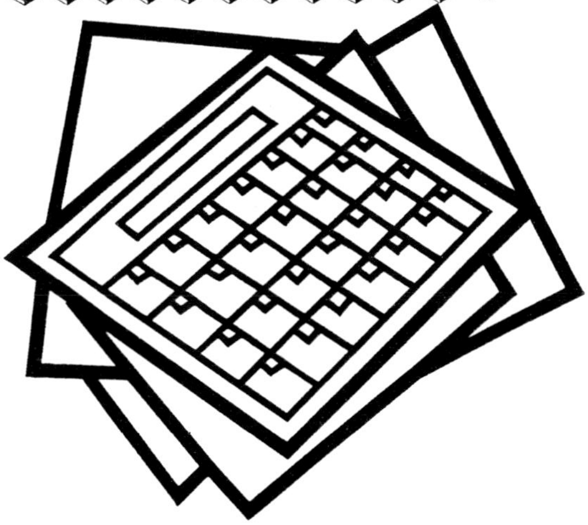

Alphabet Scavenger Hunt

An alphabet scavenger hunt can be a fun way to pass the time on any passage. Look for items that start with each letter of the alphabet aboard your boat.

Getting Underway

Goal:

Individually or in teams, try to find an item for each letter of the alphabet. The first person or team to find an item for each letter of the alphabet wins. Any item can be listed by any team but can only be listed once by that team.

Play:

To save having to stow things later, the names of the items found are written down, and everything can be kept where it was found. Each team gets a sheet of paper. Designate someone in each team to be the recorder. Before the hunt begins, each recorder lists the alphabet down the side of the paper to help keep track of what letters are needed.

Then the hunt begins. Search the boat for your letter items and write them down as you find them. When all letters are accounted for, the team signals that they are finished. The winning team is the one that finds their alphabet items first.

Variations to the Game:

A. Play with a time limit.

B. Lower the difficulty and raise the chances of success by looking for items that just have each letter of the alphabet somewhere in the word; one item for each letter. Or, play this way for only the harder letters like X or Q.

C. Raise the level of difficulty by looking for things that end with each letter of the alphabet.

Number One Rule of the Game:
ALPHABET SOUP DOES NOT COUNT!

Ideas for the Prize

A. A special treat

B. A special going ashore activity when landfall is made

C. A day off from doing dishes or cleaning up

Float an Egg

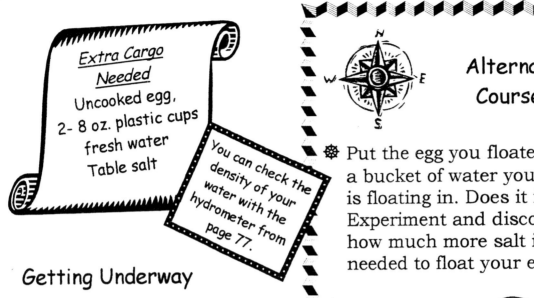

Change the density of water enough to float an egg.

Extra Cargo Needed

Uncooked egg,
2- 8 oz. plastic cups
fresh water
Table salt

You can check the density of your water with the hydrometer from page 77.

Getting Underway

Fill both of your cups ⅔ full with fresh water.

Add 3 tablespoons of salt to one of the cups and stir until completely dissolved.

First, drop the egg into the fresh water cup. What happens?

Next drop the egg into the cup with salt added. What happens?

Do ships float higher in fresh water or salt water? This is a good experiment to do before your boat goes from salt water to fresh. What do you think will happen to your waterline when you sail into fresh water from salt water or the other way around?

Alternate Courses

- Put the egg you floated into a bucket of water your boat is floating in. Does it float? Experiment and discover how much more salt is needed to float your egg.
- Try the activity with a hard boiled egg.

The Ship Watching activity on page 89 has information about how ships are loaded for salt and fresh water travel.

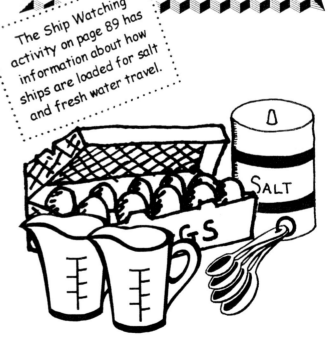

Video Journal

Video journals can be great fun because they allow a great deal of creativity. Consider filming a movie based on a particular interest or an important area you are visiting. Be a tour guide or a main character in an historical reenactment.

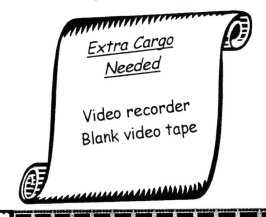

Extra Cargo Needed

Video recorder
Blank video tape

Getting Underway

Anyone that will be doing the taping should first practice the proper operation of your video equipment so they will understand how everything works. Experiment and learn how best to use the equipment.

Pick a specific topic such as the sound or picture journals discussed earlier, or record your entire voyage. If you pick a particular topic, research the subject first. Then you will be better able to narrate the action.

Videos can be as serious or as goofy as you like.

Topic Ideas

- Record a whole day trip from start to finish. Include short glimpses of packing at home, getting into the car, traveling to the boat or launching the boat, untying lines, motoring or sailing out of the harbor, and so forth. Later it is both fun and educational to watch the action at home.
- Record a day of your life aboard your boat. Send the tape to your friends or to a school so that others can learn what it's like to live aboard a boat.
- Log your trip by video.
- Make a video log of friends met or their boats underway. People love to see their own boats sailing or motoring along.

Grow a Mold Garden

It's great fun to grow your own mold garden. They are easy to start and maintain especially in the moist environment of a boat!

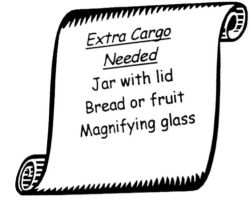

Extra Cargo Needed
- Jar with lid
- Bread or fruit
- Magnifying glass

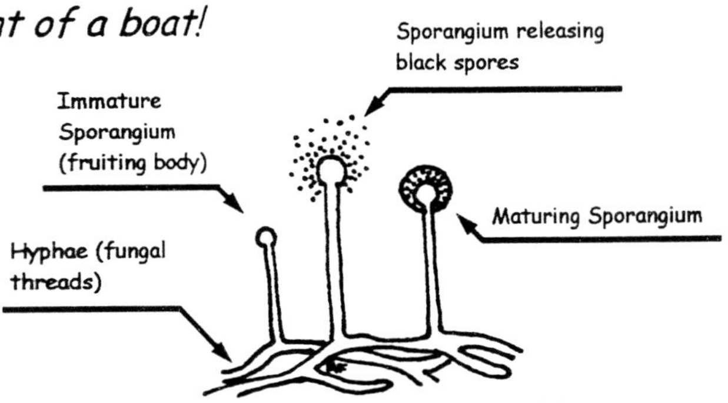

Diagram of a Pin Mold

Getting Underway

Start your mold garden by putting a piece of bread or fruit into a jar with a lid. Watch what appears after a few days. If you have a microscope or a magnifying lens you can really see what grows. Watch how the mold spreads over the food.

Draw pictures of how your mold garden changes. Describe the changes in your mold garden. Are there different kinds and colors of mold? Do they grow differently? What happens after a week? A month?

Ideas

- Grow another mold garden, but this time coat your food with something to help the mold grow quicker. Keep track of how your mold garden grows this time and compare your findings with your last mold garden.
- Here are some ideas:
  - Dip one side into milk or yogurt.
  - Coat your food with honey or sugar. Or, coat it with honey on one half and sugar on the other half.
  - Spread peanut butter on one half and jelly on the other.
- Have a mold growing competition!
- Try things that might inhibit mold growth like vinegar, lime juice, lemon juice, or salt.

Monitoring Whales

Record the cetacean sightings on your boating trips. You can even help monitor whale and sea life for research organizations. See the next activity for more information.

Getting Underway

Each time a whale is sighted record the general position using your dead reckoning position or GPS position. Other things to record:

- Time
- Weather
- Number of cetaceans
- Their behavior

You can plot the sightings directly on your chart or record the information in a tracking journal by photocopying one of the tracking sheets from Compartment A of the Cargo Hold. See page 171 to order our inexpensive Marine Animal Tracking Journal.

Fin whales are fast swimmers, reaching speeds of up to 19 mph.

Ideas

- In the same general area, tow your plankton net (to make one see page 41) to see if they were attracted to high levels of plankton in the water. Some cetaceans may be attracted to the fish that are attracted to the plankton in the water.
- Draw pictures of the cetaceans you see or take pictures and put them in your journal.

Cetaceans are the scientific family that include whales, dolphins, and porpoises.

Sperm whales dive deepest of all whales. The deepest dive recorded is 6,560 feet by one male sperm whale in the Caribbean.

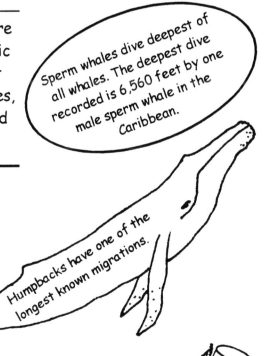

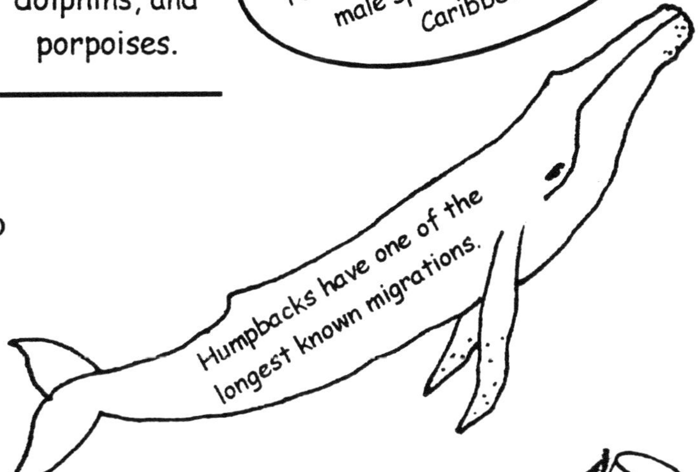

Humpbacks have one of the longest known migrations.

Alternate Courses

- Monitor other animals besides cetaceans. Consider keeping track of the different kinds and numbers of sea birds, sea turtles, seals and sea lions, or manatees you see. Document the numbers and kinds of animals you see during your boating excursions. It will give you an idea of the health of the environment you are exploring and may end up helping scientific research. Look in Compartment A of the Cargo Hold for tracking sheets to photocopy.
- Share the information you learn about cetaceans with other interested people.

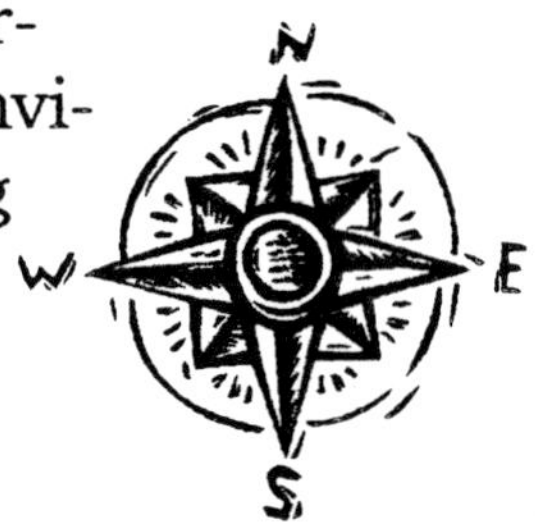

WATCH OUT! When viewing whales, always give them plenty of space to maneuver and leave the area. Never approach too closely! See page 149 for whale watching guidelines. WATCH OUT!

Northern Right Whales have special protection because of their endangered status. It is against the law to approach them within 500 yards.

Look in Compartment B of The Cargo Hold for a short identification guide to common whales and dolphins.

Monitor Cetaceans for Science

Here is the contact information for three organizations that would like to receive information about cetacean sightings.

Getting Underway

The first step in helping these organizations is to contact them and request information about their whale watching program for volunteer observers. Each organization uses its own form to report data, so you will need to request copies of this as well.

There are several organizations that would be interested in receiving information about cetacean sightings. Here are addresses for two organizations that need volunteer monitors:

WHALEFORCE
c/o Cochrane Ecological Institute
P.O. Box 484
Cochrane, AB
Canada T0L 0W0
E-mail: cei@cadvision.com
Website: www.ceinst.org

International Dolphin Watch
10 Melton Road
North Ferriby, East Yorkshire
HU14 3ET England
E-mail: dolphincity@dial.pipex.com

WhaleNet

WhaleNet is an educational website as well as a clearinghouse for cetacean research on the Internet. It focuses on whales, the marine habitat, and environmental studies. Many cetacean research organizations can be reached through this information clearinghouse. The people of WhaleNet would be interested in staying in touch with cruising families and gaining observations from those families as they travel. They have a volunteer monitoring program for people who want to monitor cetacean sightings and water pollution. Visit their website:
http://whale.wheelock.edu

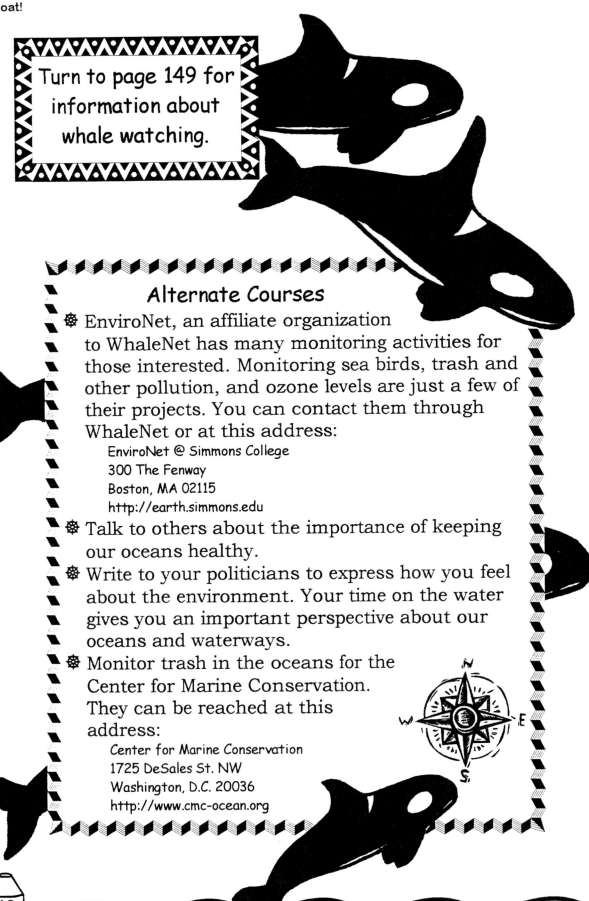

Turn to page 149 for information about whale watching.

Alternate Courses

- EnviroNet, an affiliate organization to WhaleNet has many monitoring activities for those interested. Monitoring sea birds, trash and other pollution, and ozone levels are just a few of their projects. You can contact them through WhaleNet or at this address:

  EnviroNet @ Simmons College
  300 The Fenway
  Boston, MA 02115
  http://earth.simmons.edu

- Talk to others about the importance of keeping our oceans healthy.
- Write to your politicians to express how you feel about the environment. Your time on the water gives you an important perspective about our oceans and waterways.
- Monitor trash in the oceans for the Center for Marine Conservation. They can be reached at this address:

  Center for Marine Conservation
  1725 DeSales St. NW
  Washington, D.C. 20036
  http://www.cmc-ocean.org

Make a Plankton Net

Make your own plankton net for catching plankton on boating trips and sample tiny marine life in the waters around your boat.

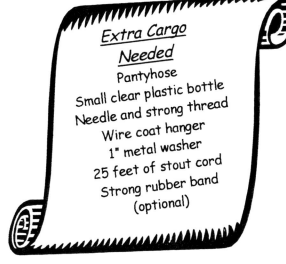

Extra Cargo Needed

Pantyhose
Small clear plastic bottle
Needle and strong thread
Wire coat hanger
1" metal washer
25 feet of stout cord
Strong rubber band (optional)

Getting Underway

Step 1

Make a 7½-inch diameter (23½-inch circumference) circle with some of the wire from the coat hanger. Protect the sharp edges with seizing or strong tape.

Step 1.

Step 2

Cut one of the legs off the pantyhose. That cut-off leg will become your plankton net. Sew the opening of the leg onto the wire ring using small stitches.

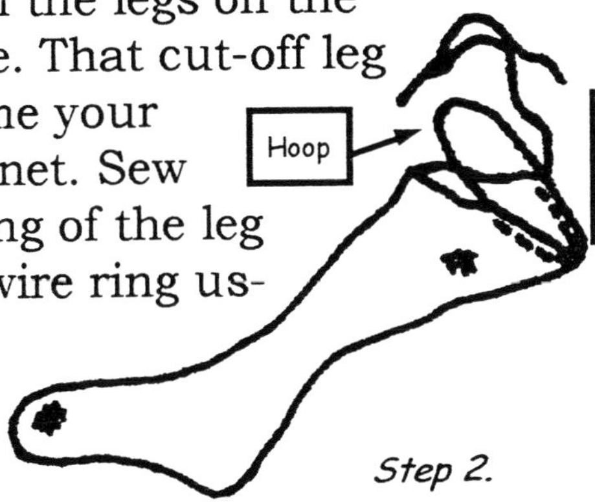

Step 2.

Step 3

Put the small bottle into the foot of the stocking and position it so that the open end is facing the opening of the stocking. Then tie in place with a little of the cord or with a strong rubber band.

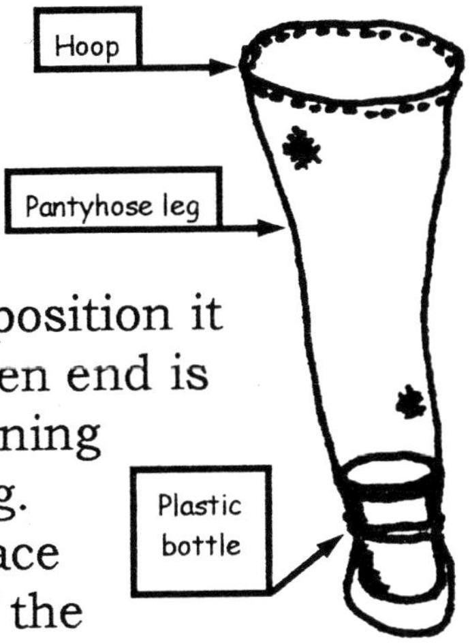

Step 3.

Step 4

Tie three 2-ft. lengths of cord to the washer.

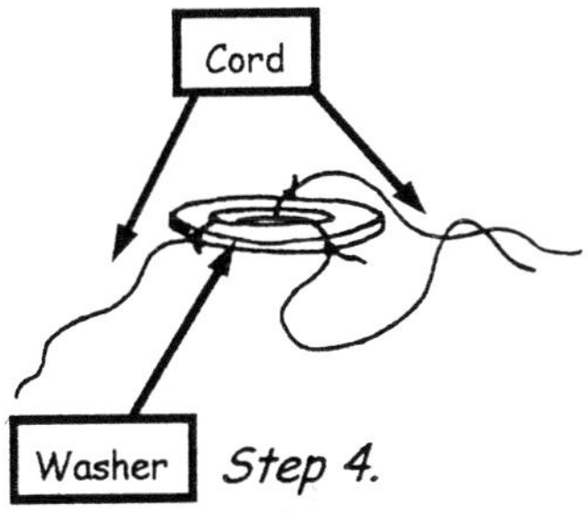

Step 4.

Step 5

Now, create a bridle by tying the free ends of the three lengths of cord to the hoop under or through the pantyhose. Then, attach 15-20 feet of the cord to the washer.

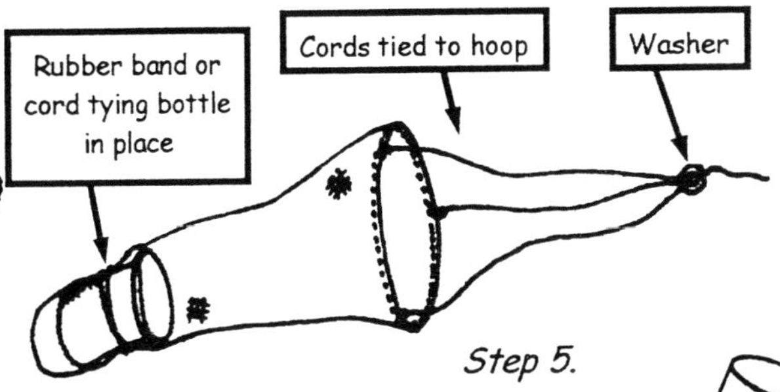

Step 5.

Using your Plankton Net

Sample the waters around your boat or dinghy with your own plankton net. What strange little creatures will you find?

Extra Cargo Needed

Field microscope or magnifying glass

Plankton identification guide in Compartment B of Cargo Hold

Getting Underway

Tow your plankton net during a time when you are traveling slowly. Your dinghy also works great for this. Try not to catch large pieces of seaweed or other items that may stretch the net and cause it to rip. As you tow it behind your boat, it will gather more and more creatures and the water will flow through and spill out the sides. After a few minutes, carefully bring your net aboard trying to keep the vial upright so that you will get a full bottle of water to investigate. Drip a few drops of this water onto a plate. Look at your catch with your magnifying glass or field microscope. Sample the water in several locations.

Plankton

Plankton are small freshwater and marine organisms that live mostly on or near the surface of water. They drift with currents and tides because they are too weak or too small to propel themselves through waves and currents.

There are two major kinds of plankton; *Phytoplankton* produce their own food through photosynthesis and *zooplankton* which prey on the phytoplankton. Plankton also consists of eggs and larvae of larger species of fresh and salt water animals and plants.

Look for a helpful plankton identification guide in the Cargo Hold.

Make a reusable line for all of your research tools on page 63.

If you don't have one already, consider buying a field microscope to bring aboard when you travel. They are small, fairly rugged, and magnify objects better than a simple magnifying glass. Some even have lights so that you can see the object better. Look for them in educational toy stores.

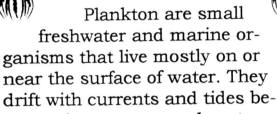

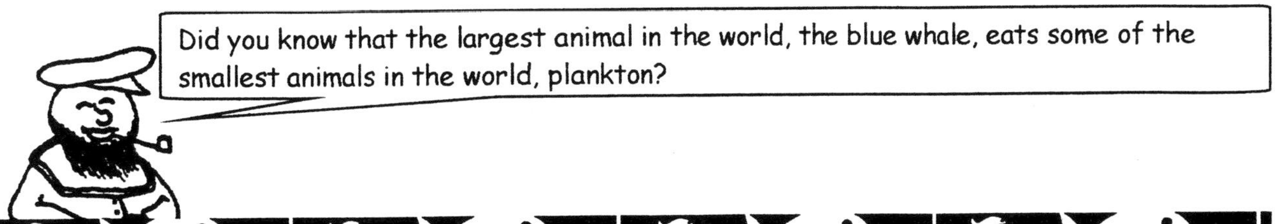

Did you know that the largest animal in the world, the blue whale, eats some of the smallest animals in the world, plankton?

Ideas

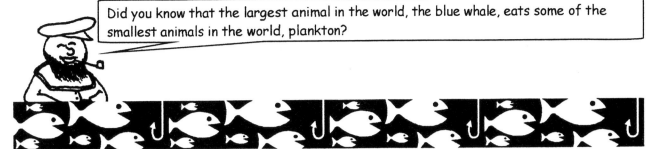

- Take water samples periodically as you travel to different anchorages or places. Look at these samples with your magnifying glass or field microscope. Do the number of organisms increase as you get closer to a city? Do the kinds of animals change? Can you identify any of the creatures?
- Bring along a book about microscopic creatures on one of your trips so that you can identify and learn about these creatures that most people never consider outside of biology class.
- Draw pictures of the creatures you find, make note of how they move through the water. Then watch and find out how they eat. Does the food come to them or do they hunt for it?
- Start a journal to record your findings.
- Tow it just before you fish and check the amount of plankton in relation to the amount of fish caught.
- If you monitor whale sightings, tow your plankton net each time you sight a whale or dolphin. Record your findings along with your whale tracking information.

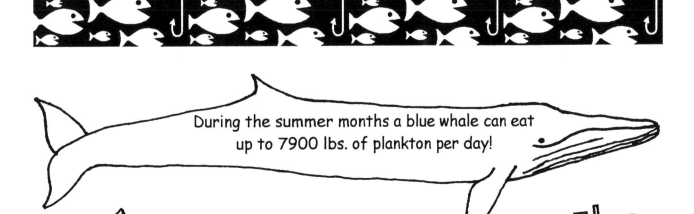

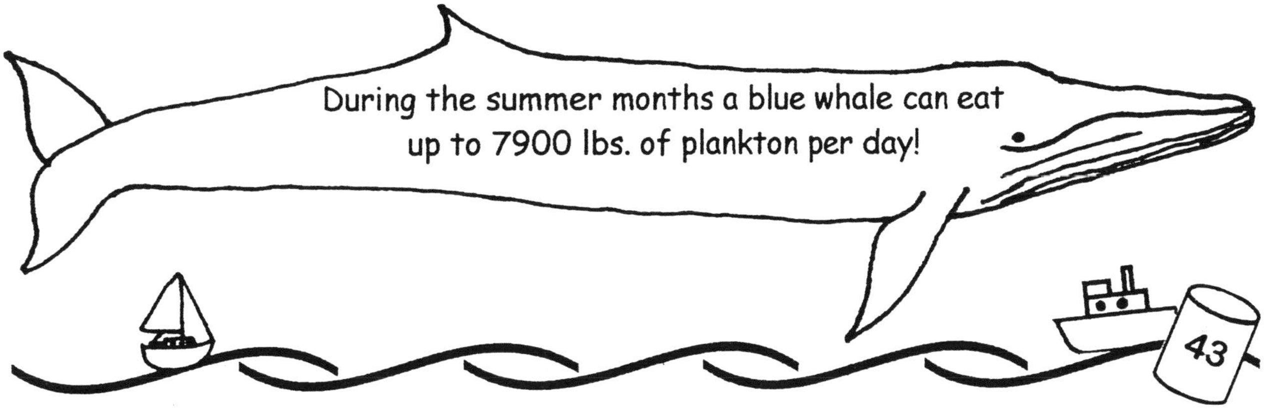

During the summer months a blue whale can eat up to 7900 lbs. of plankton per day!

Water Pressure Experimentation

Use an empty plastic bottle to experiment with and learn about water pressure.

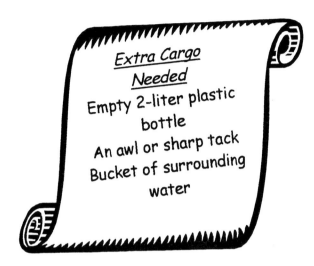

Extra Cargo Needed

Empty 2-liter plastic bottle
An awl or sharp tack
Bucket of surrounding water

Getting Underway

Outside on the deck, carefully punch a hole about an inch from the top of the bottle. Fill the bottle to the top with water and observe the water pour from the hole. Empty the bottle. Now punch two more holes, each at a different level of the bottle being careful not to collapse the bottle. Fill the bottle full again. Observe how the water pressure increases with water depth. The deeper the hole, the more forceful the stream of water escaping.

Alternate Courses

- While doing this experiment, hold your finger over each hole to feel the difference in force.
- If you are a swimmer, the next time you dive into the water to swim, feel for water pressure. The deeper you go, the more water pressure you feel pushing on you, especially your ears.

The water coming from the lower holes squirts out with more force because of the increased water pressure caused by the added weight as the water depth increases.

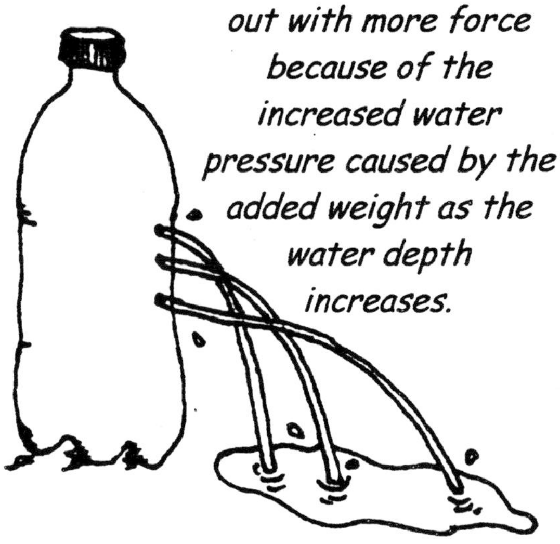

Make a Secchi Disk

Oceanographers use a secchi (pronounced sek-ee) disk to measure the clarity of the water. You can easily make your own. Then you can find out how far you can see into the water

Extra Cargo Needed

White disc (plastic plate or Frisbee®)
Drill
90 feet non-floating line
2-3 medium lead fishing weights
Measuring tape

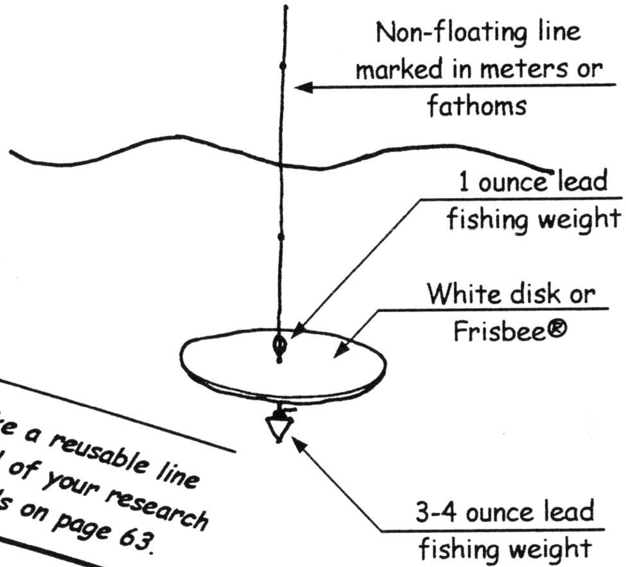

Make a reusable line for all of your research tools on page 63.

Getting Underway

Step 1

Drill a whole in the center of your white disc large enough so that the non-floating line will pass through. To find the disc's center, see the next page.

Step 2

Thread the line through the disk with medium lead weights attached on either side. Put a stopper knot, like a figure eight knot, at the end.

Step 3

Mark the line every six-feet (fathom) or every meter. You are done!

Using your Secchi Disk

While the boat is not moving, lower your secchi disc into the water and watch until it is no longer visible. Count the marks at the waterline as you bring in the line. The number of meters or fathoms tells you how far you can see into the water.

Check the clarity at different times and during different conditions in the same place. How does a cloudy day affect your reading? A river close by? A breaking reef close by?

Finding the center of your Disc

If your disc has no center marked, trace around your disk on a piece of paper, then cut it out. Fold your circle in half, then in half again making sharp creases. Unfold and make a mark with a marker where the folds meet up. Now tape the paper onto your disc and use that mark to guide you with your drilling.

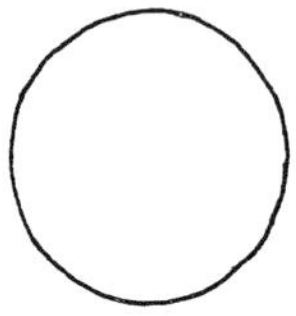

Fig. 1. Disc traced and cut out

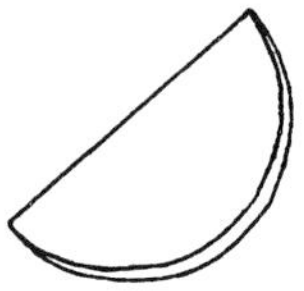

Fig. 2. Circle folded in half

Fig 3. Circle folded in half again

Salinity, turbulence, amount of silt and debris in the water, and the amount of sunlight will affect your readings.

Your secchi disk's white color helps you to see it better in any water.

Alternate Courses

- Use your secchi disk whenever you spot a whale or dolphin. Record the water clarity along with your whale sighting information.
- Record the water clarity in your anchorage journal or marina journal whenever you stop somewhere new.

If you fish, use heavy duty fishing line for your secchi disk line. Just make a loop with a small amount of line on your secchi disk. Then attach your fishing line to the loop with a strong opening swivel. Mark the line at six-foot (or meter) intervals. Now your fishing pole has two uses.

97% of the earth's water is in the oceans.

Japanese Fish Printing

Printing is an important art form in Japanese culture. Experiment with printing the next time you catch a fish.

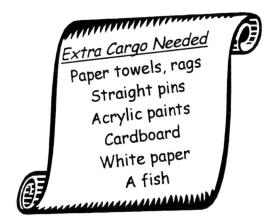

Extra Cargo Needed

- Paper towels, rags
- Straight pins
- Acrylic paints
- Cardboard
- White paper
- A fish

Getting Underway

Step 1

First, gently dry the fish with paper towels or rags being careful not to wipe off any scales.

Step 2

Lay the fish on a large piece of cardboard.

Step 3

Pin out the fish's fins with straight pins along the edges of the fins so that the fins will stay spread out. Cut out the eyes and wedge a little bit of rolled up paper towel into the socket. Let the fish dry for 30 min. to an hour.

Step 4

With acrylic paint, paint the fish all over on one side. Move it onto a clean piece of newspaper. Have a piece of printing paper ready.

Step 5

Carefully press the paper onto the fish. Mold it to the fish being careful **not** to move the paper along the fish, or it will smear the print. Use a paper that has a soft feel. Rice paper is ideal. Stiff paper is harder to work with.

Step 6

Try again with a second piece of paper. Usually the second printing will come out better because the paint will have spread into cracks and crevices in the fish's body showing more texture.

Step 7

Let your prints dry in a safe place away from weather.

The first printing can lack texture.

The paint settles in with the second printing and reveals more of the fish.

Alternate Courses

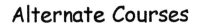

- Try this technique to make unique T-shirts. Use the T-shirt in place of the paper in the printing process. Acrylic paints work well for this.
- Make printings of other things like shells and dried seaweed.
- With thicker paper, make holiday cards with printings to send to family and friends.

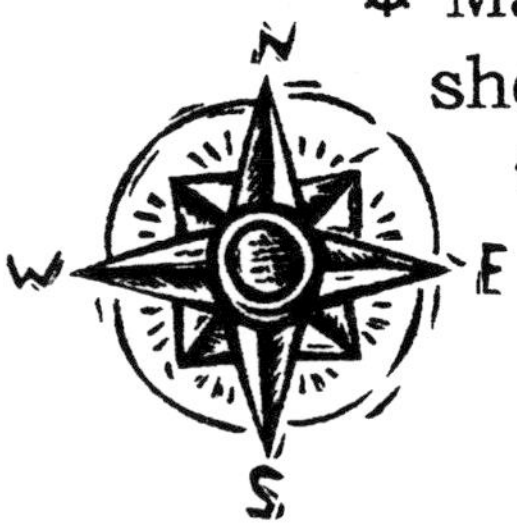

Send home a bit of your trip to family and friends!

Fish Dissection

Identify and dissect the fish you catch. Parental supervision is required for this activity.

Extra Cargo Needed

- Fillet knife
- Sharp craft knife
- Tooth picks
- Cutting board
- Newspaper
- Magnifying glass

Be careful of any sharp spines on your fish!

Getting Underway

After catching a fish and filleting it, explore the remains. Lay out several layers of newspaper and your cutting board where you will be working.

Use toothpicks to poke and prod, the small knife for cutting into organs to investigate, and your magnifying glass to see detail.

Identify the organs and separate them for inspection. If you have a reference book on fish, use it as you explore. It is especially interesting to cut into the stomach to see what the fish had been eating. Make sure you wash your hands when you are done!

The **lateral line** on a fish contain sensory organs that allow the fish to maintain its balance, detect vibrations, plus changes in temperature and pressure.

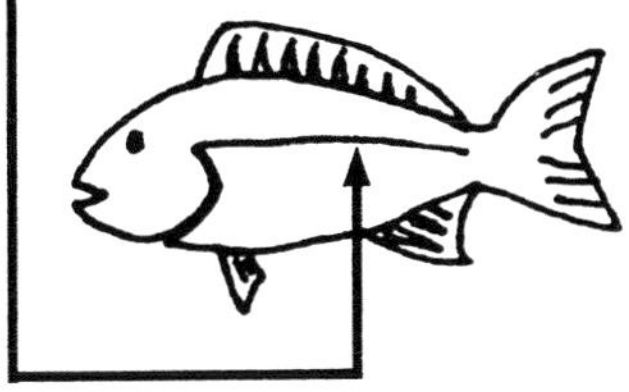

Anatomy of a Bony Fish

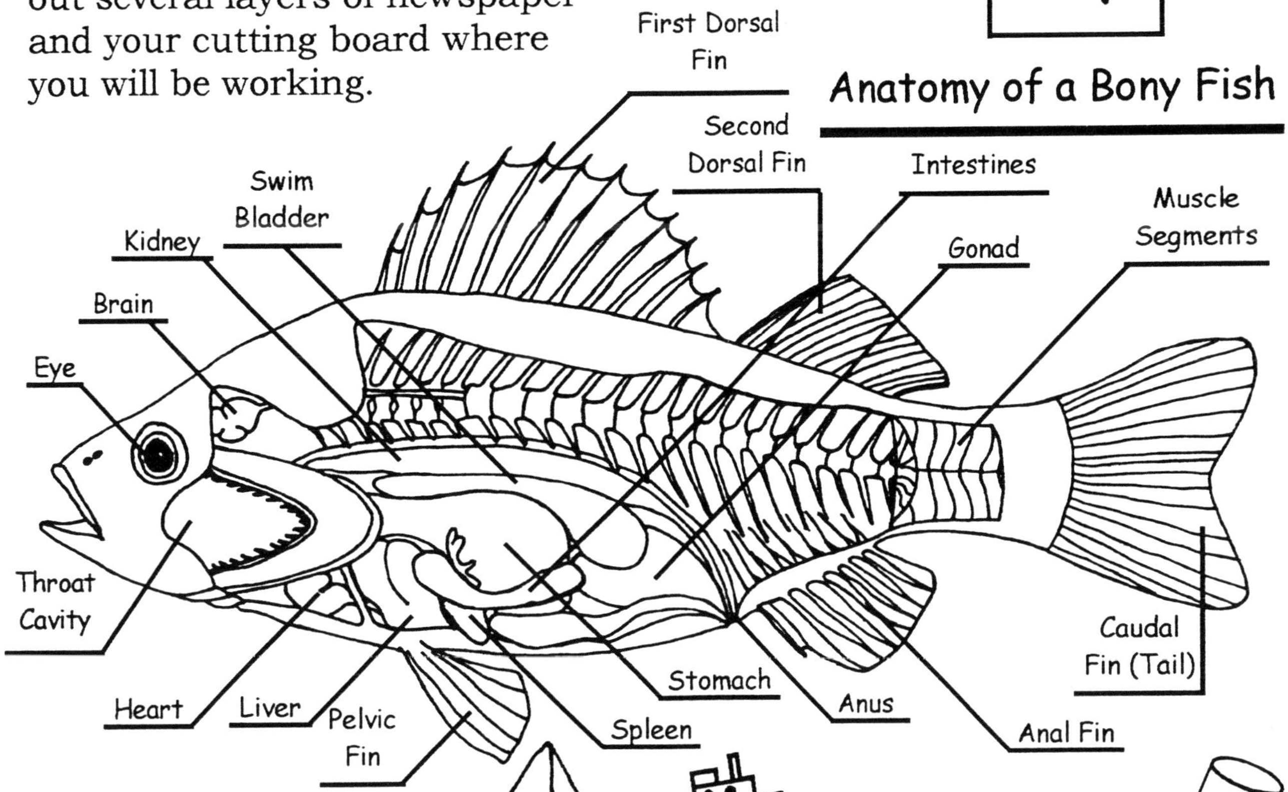

Salt Crystal Pictures

Make salt crystal pictures by drawing with salt water on black construction paper.

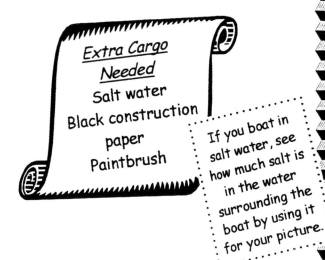

Extra Cargo Needed

Salt water
Black construction paper
Paintbrush

If you boat in salt water, see how much salt is in the water surrounding the boat by using it for your picture.

Getting Underway

Dip your fingers, paintbrush, sticks, forks, etc. into a bowl of salt water. Draw a picture with the salt water on black construction paper.

Actually, any color construction paper can be used, but the darker the paper the more easily the salt will show. Let your picture dry outside in the sun on a calm day, or inside the boat cabin if it is windy.

When the water evaporates, the salt remains to make the picture you drew.

Alternate Courses

- When boating in salt water, try leaving a small amount of seawater in a dish in the sink or in the cockpit. Make note of the time and day. Try to guess how many hours or days it will take to evaporate.
- Dip the whole piece of black construction paper into the salt water then let it dry in a quiet place away from any drafts. When dry, use your fingernail to etch a picture into the salty covering.

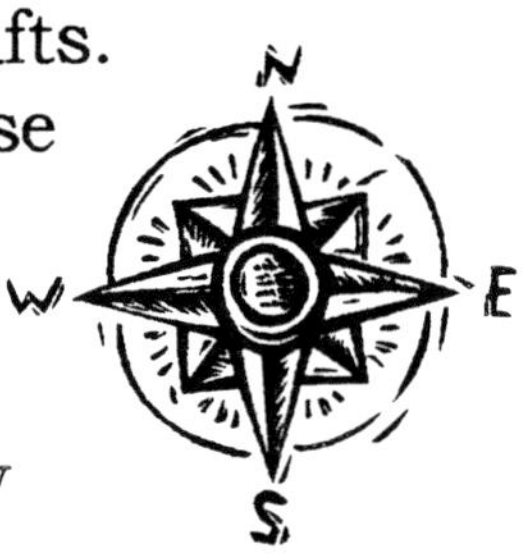

Water in the ocean is about 3.5 % salt.

Make your own Sounding Lead

It's easy to make your own depth sounder! It can become a boat saver if your electronic depth sounder ever fails to function.

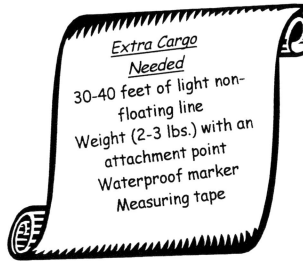

Extra Cargo Needed

30-40 feet of light non-floating line
Weight (2-3 lbs.) with an attachment point
Waterproof marker
Measuring tape

Getting Underway

Making your own sounding lead is as simple as attaching your weight to one end of your line with a sturdy knot. Then mark your line at 6-foot (one-fathom) or one-meter intervals. You've made your own sounding lead!

Any fairly heavy object can be used as your weight for your sounding lead. It only needs to have a place to attach your line. A dimpled surface helps if you will be putting peanut butter or gum on the bottom of the weight to check the bottom's composition.

Using your Sounding Lead

At anchor or the dock, find the depth of the water by lowering your weight into the water. Let the line slide through your fingers. Be careful not to release all the line! When you can no longer feel the weight of your sounding lead, your weight has hit bottom. Count the marks from the *waterline* as you bring your sounding lead back aboard your boat to find out how many fathoms or meters deep the water is.

Compare your findings with an electronic depth sounder. The reading you get from your electronic depth sounder may need to be adjusted depending on where the transducer is mounted on your boat.

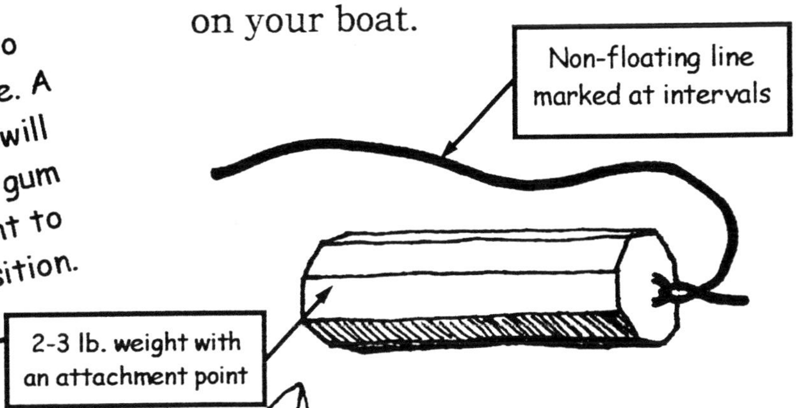

WATCH OUT! Be careful not to throw your sounding lead near people or breakable objects.

The Mariana Trench, a deep sea valley stretching 1554 miles long with an average width of 44 miles is famous for the deepest depression on Earth. Called the Challenger Deep, it is 36,198 feet deep.

The deepest descent into the sea was made in 1960 by the bathyscaphe, *Trieste*. That submersible took its crew down 35,810 feet!

Make a reusable line for all of your research tools on page 63.

Alternate Courses

- Spread peanut butter or stick a bit of chewed gum on the bottom of your sounding lead to get a sample of the bottom.
- Attach a strong magnet to some line and see what comes up!

N
W
E
S

Charts use these abbreviations for the common types of seafloors found.

Nautical Abbreviations for Types of Seabed			
S	Sand	*Cb*	Cobbles
M	Mud	*R; Rk; Rky*	Rocky
Cy ; Cl	Clay	*Co*	Coral; Coral-line algae
Si	Silt	*Sh*	Shells
St	Stones	*S/M*	Sand over Mud, Two layers
G	Gravel	*Wd*	Weed (including Kelp)
P	Pebbles	*Grs*	Grass

Bottom Topography

On one of your trips, make a graph of the changes the sea floor goes through.

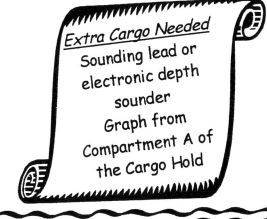

Extra Cargo Needed
Sounding lead or electronic depth sounder
Graph from Compartment A of the Cargo Hold

Getting Underway

While underway, use your depth sounder or sounding lead (if shallow enough) and record your depth on the graph every nautical mile. How do you know when you have traveled a nautical mile? Go to the activity named "Find your Speed through the Water," on page 21. Find your speed then divide 60 minutes by your speed in knots to find out how many minutes it takes to travel one nautical mile.

Now you have the time between depth recordings. If your speed is greater than 10 knots, lengthen the distance and time between recordings and change the scale of the graph along both sides.

Topography Example

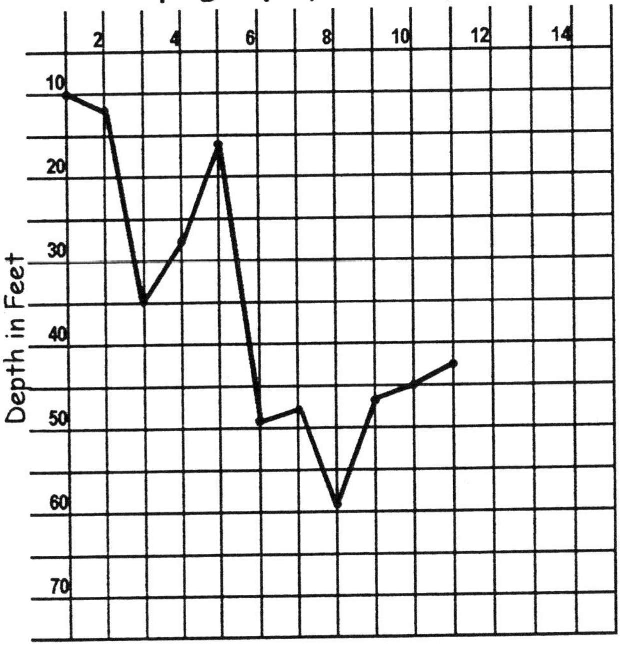

Nautical Miles Traveled

Figure 1.

Depth	N. Miles
10 ft.	1
12 ft.	2
35 ft.	3
28 ft.	4
16 ft.	5
49 ft.	6
48 ft.	7
59 ft.	8
47 ft.	9
45 ft.	10
43 ft.	11

Figure 2.

The graph in figure 1 above shows how you would chart the sample recordings in figure 2. Make note that the depth is in feet and in descending order from the top in order to better illustrate the bottom topography recorded.

Make your own sounding lead on page 51!

Alternate Courses

- You can do this activity in an anchorage using your dinghy and a handheld GPS for speed and distance figures. You will need to use a different scale, such as measuring the depth every 100 feet.
- If you chose to use your sounding lead from page 51, put peanut butter or chewed gum on the bottom of the weight before sending it down. A sample of the bottom will come up with your lead. Then record the type of bottom you travel over. Is it the same as the chart?
- As you travel over different types of bottoms, mark where it changes on the graph.

The Ocean Floor

The ocean floor is as varied and full of features as the land of each of our continents.

Except for international boat traffic, most boating occurs over the continental shelf.

(Picture not drawn to scale)

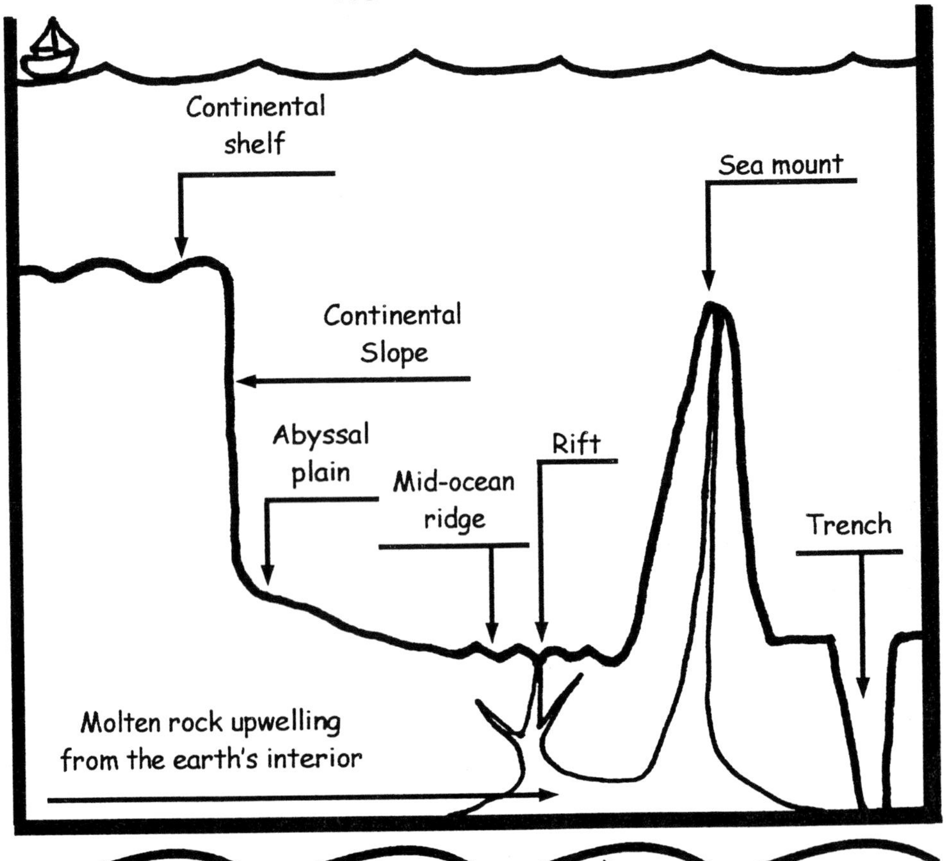

Make an Anemometer

Make your own handheld anemometer to measure the wind's strength. The straw handle lets you move to different places onboard to check the wind.

Extra Cargo Needed

- 4 Small disposable cups
- Long galvanized nail
- 3 Drinking straws
- Stapler
- Tape
- Bright colored paper

Getting Underway

First, find and mark the center of 2 of the straws. Use your galvanized nail to carefully puncture a hole through each marked straw. See figure 1.

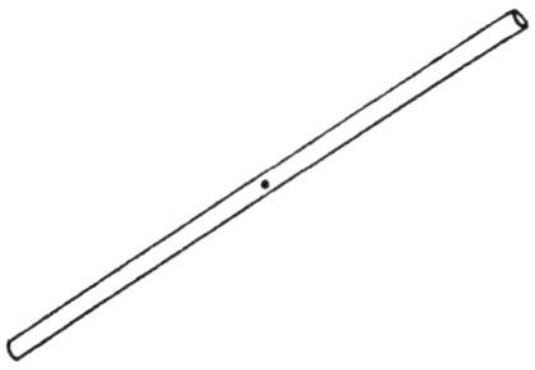

Figure 1.

Pinching one of these straws in the middle with both hands, move one hand along one length of the straw flattening it as you move. Keeping it pinched at the end, grab a cup and mold the flattened straw along the drinking edge for a few inches with the cup facing you. Staple the straw to the cup. See figure 2.

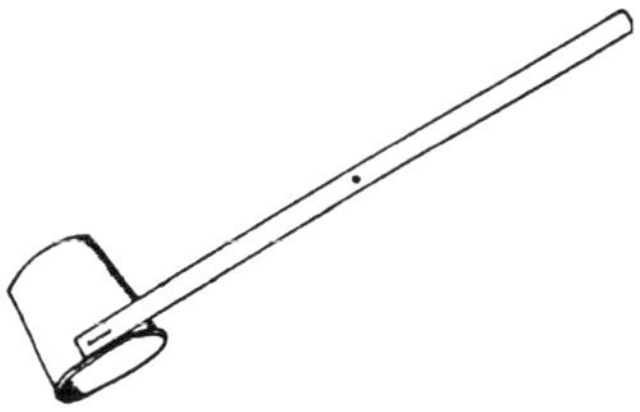

Figure 2.

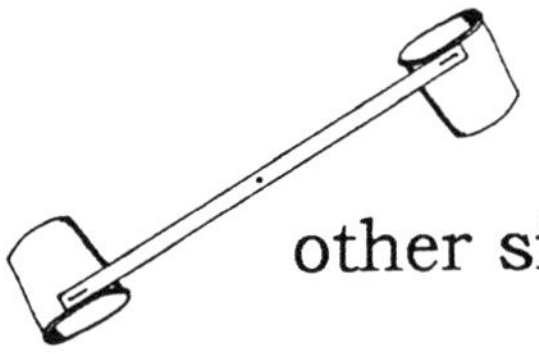

Figure 3.

Flattening the straw along the other side and molding it a few inches along the drinking edge of another cup, staple the straw to the cup with the cup facing away from you. See figure 3. Make the same cup/straw arrangement with the other marked straw. Be careful to keep the straw flattened along the same edge as you staple the cups so that they are level when stapled.

Thread the 2 straw/cup arrangements onto the nail and spread them apart so that the straws are perpendicular. The cups should face towards the same direction as you look at them in a circle. See figure 4.

Glue the two straws together so that they cannot move away from perpendicular. Let dry.

Now place the nail inside the third straw as a handle. You've made your anemometer!

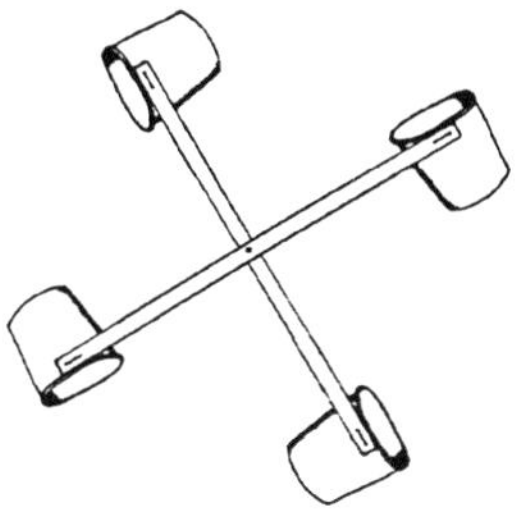

Figure 4.

Calibrating and Using Your Anemometer

Glue or tape a strip of brightly colored paper on the edge of one of the cups so that it sticks out or up slightly.

Check the wind conditions using the Beaufort scale on this page or using a boat's anemometer. Watch your anemometer turn in the wind.

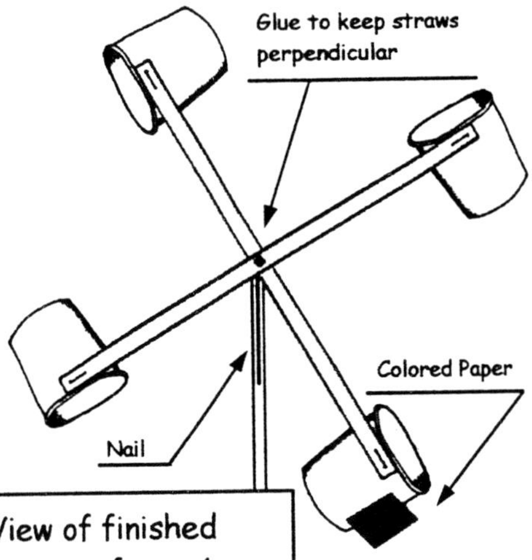

View of finished anemometer from above.

Count the number of times the paper strip passes your nose or arm in 10 seconds. Then, multiply this number by 6 to get the revolutions per minute.

Compare that number to the wind strength you found at first to calibrate your anemometer. Test it in different wind strengths.

Beaufort Scale of Wind Strength

Sea State Observed	International Description	Beaufort #	MPH	Knots
Sea glassy	Calm	0	<1	<1
Ripples with the appearance of scales and no foam crests	Light air	1	1-3	1-3
Small wavelets, crests have a glassy appearance, no breaking waves	Light breeze	2	4-7	4-6
Large wavelets; crests begin to break with scattered whitecaps	Gentle Breeze	3	8-12	7-10
Small waves ($\frac{1}{2}$-$1\frac{1}{4}$ meters) becoming larger; numerous whitecaps	Moderate	4	13-18	11-16
Moderate waves ($1\frac{1}{4}$-$2\frac{1}{2}$ meters) taking longer form; many whitecaps; some spray	Fresh	5	19-24	17-21
Larger waves ($2\frac{1}{2}$-4 meters); whitecaps everywhere; more spray	Strong	6	25-31	22-27
Sea heaps, waves 4-6 meters; white foam from breaking waves begin to blow in streaks	Near Gale	7	32-38	28-33
Waves 4-6 meters becoming greater in length; edge of crests begin to break into spindrift; foam blown in well marked streaks	Gale	8	39-46	34-40
Waves 6 meters, sea begins to roll; dense streaks of foam; spray may reduce visibility	Strong Gale	9	47-54	41-47
Waves 6-9 meters with overhanging crests; sea takes a white appearance as foam is blown in dense streaks; rolling is heavy; visibility is reduced	Storm	10	55-63	48-55
Waves 9-14 meters; sea covered with white foam patches and visibility reduced more	Violent Storm	11	64-73	56-63
Waves over 14 meters; air filled with foam; sea completely white with driving spray; visibility greatly reduced	Hurricane	12	74-82	64-71

Make a Rain Gauge

Without measuring, it's difficult to tell just how much rain came from that last storm. Measure the amount of rainfall properly with your own rain gauge!

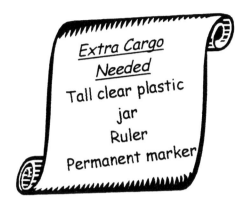

Extra Cargo Needed

- Tall clear plastic jar
- Ruler
- Permanent marker

Getting Underway

Using your ruler as a guide, mark the jar from the bottom up at $\frac{1}{4}$ or $\frac{1}{2}$-inch intervals. To stop the ruler from moving around on the jar, temporarily tape it to the jar.

Place your jar outside on the boat somewhere where it won't be easily spilled. It can be hung in the rigging with a couple of holes drilled through the top and some string or light weight line to tie it down.

At the end of each day, measure the rainfall, then empty the gauge. Checking it at the same time each day will give you an accurate reading over the last 24 hours.

Helpful Hints

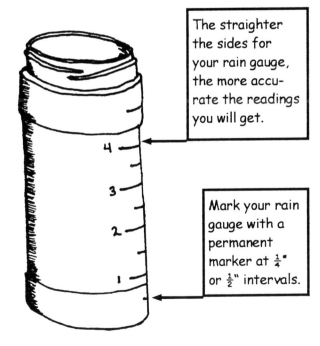

Cylindrical jars work best for rain gauges. Their straight sides and wide mouth will give you a more accurate reading of the amounts of rain.

Tall spice jars or plastic peanut butter jars work well as a rain gauge since they have wide mouths, are usually cylindrical, and clear.

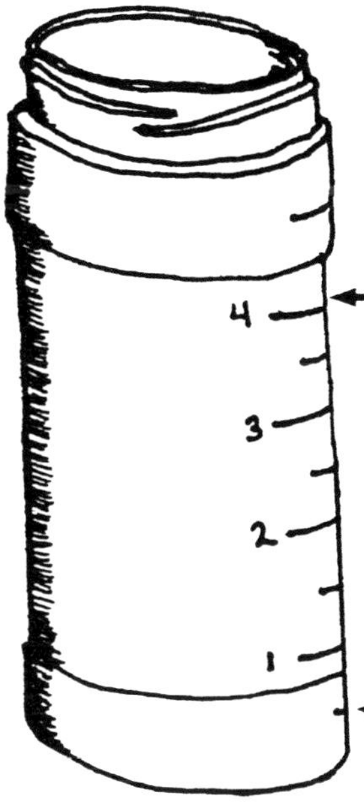

The straighter the sides for your rain gauge, the more accurate the readings you will get.

Mark your rain gauge with a permanent marker at $\frac{1}{4}$" or $\frac{1}{2}$" intervals.

Make a Thermometer

Build your own bottle thermometer. Watch how it shows the temperature changes on board your boat.

<u>Extra Cargo Needed</u>

- Tap water
- Rubbing alcohol
- Food coloring
- Clear bottle
- Clear plastic straw
- Modeling clay

A medium sized narrow mouthed bottle like an 11 ounce drinking water bottle works well.

The alcohol/water mixture expands as it gets warmer. Since there is no other place for the liquid to go, it rises inside the straw the same way it does in any thermometer.

Watch your thermometer throughout the day. But, be careful not to let it heat up so much that the liquid spills out of the top of the straw!

Wedge your thermometer somewhere safe when you are underway!

Getting Underway

Fill your bottle $\frac{1}{4}$ full with a mixture of 50% tap water and 50% rubbing alcohol. Remember this type of alcohol is lethal, DO NOT DRINK IT!! Add a few drops of food coloring to this mixture.

Place your straw into the bottle being careful not to let it touch the bottom of the bottle. Seal the mouth of the bottle with modeling clay so that it is air tight around the straw and holds the straw in place.

Now, hold the base of the bottle in your hands to warm it up. Watch what happens.

WATCH OUT! When you are done with your thermometer, be sure to dispose of your bottle and alcohol mixture properly. The bottle cannot be reused.

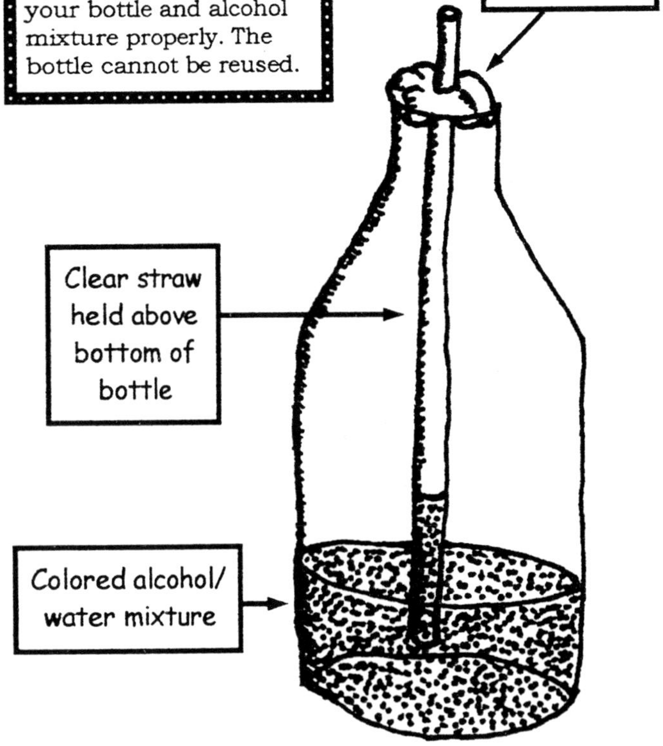

Track the Weather

Weather is very important in boating. Learn about weather patterns and forecasting by keeping track of the weather.

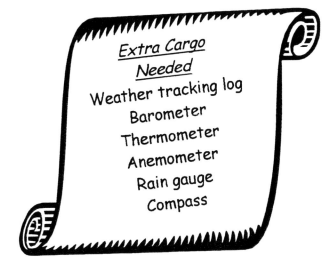

Extra Cargo Needed

Weather tracking log
Barometer
Thermometer
Anemometer
Rain gauge
Compass

Getting Underway

Track the weather in a weather log twice a day at about the same times. Record the following in the log:

- Temperature
- Percentage of cloud cover
- Types of clouds
- Barometric pressure
- Approximate visibility
- Wind speed
- Wind direction
- Wave height if at sea
- Rainfall amounts if you have a gauge

Ideas

- Simplify the tracking by recording the temperature, basic weather (sunny, cloudy, rainy), rainfall amount, and time on a calendar.
- After recording the weather for one area for several months, calculate the percentage of sunny or rainy days.
- If you are traveling long distances, you will be able to watch climatic changes as you travel.

Make your own rain gauge on page 57.

Look in Compartment A of the Cargo Hold for weather tracking logs that you can photocopy. Or you can order our Weather Tracking Journal on page 171. Also look for a guide to clouds in Cargo Hold B.

Buys-Ballot Law

In the Northern Hemisphere, "Face the wind to find the low pressure center to your right." In the Southern Hemisphere, "Face the wind to find the low pressure center to your left."

Russia's Vostok station in Antarctica typically records the lowest yearly air temperatures. Recorded in late August, usually the lowest temperature recorded is around -126°F.
Now that's COLD!!

Alternate Courses

☸ Watch and track weather systems on your chart as they approach. During hurricane or typhoon season, track the tropical systems on a world map. Include information about the wind speeds and size of the systems.

☸ If you are interested in meteorology, get a book about weather forecasting. Add your forecast to the weather log and calculate your percentage of correct forecasting.

Waialeale peak on the island of Kauai, Hawaii is one of the wettest places in the world. It receives 460 inches of rain a year!

Nautical Weather Lore

When boat horns sound hollow,
Rain will surely follow.

Mackerel skies and mare's tails
Make tall ships carry low sails.

Winds that swing against the sun
And winds that bring the rain are one.
Winds that swing with the sun
Keep the rain storm on the run.

Changing Scenes

Draw or paint the same scene in the early morning, then again in the late afternoon. What changes do you see?

Extra Cargo Needed

Colored pencils, markers or water based paints

Getting Underway

Pick a pretty scene from your boat while you are at anchor or at a dock. Draw it at different times during the day such as the morning, late afternoon, at sunset, or at dawn.

Compare how the shadows are different. Compare how the colors are different.

On the back of each picture make note of the time and date.

Alternate Courses

- Try this activity using your camera to take pictures of the changing scene. Be as accurate as possible when matching up the same scene.
- If you do this activity close to your home port, create drawings or paintings of the same scene for each season of the year.

Draw the same scene at different times of the day!

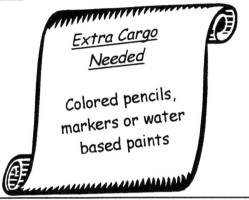

Late morning

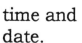

Sunrise

Litter Art

Create a work of art from castaway treasures in your own trash can or from litter found in the water while you boat.

Extra Cargo Needed

Long handled net
Litter
Craft glue or super glue
Scissors

When you are finished with your creations, remember to dispose of them properly!

Getting Underway

Gather litter with a long handled net while traveling slowly through the water or use your own trash or castaways to create a litter sculpture or picture. If you gather litter from the water, try to pick pieces that have been washed clean by the water. Also, be careful of sharp pieces of litter.

Spread newspaper down where you are working to minimize the clean up later.

Wind, waves, and the sun can create strange effects on the litter you find. Look at the colors, shapes, and textures of your litter to get an idea of how to use each piece. Glue your pieces together and let dry thoroughly.

With large plastic or wooden pieces, it may be better to use brads along with glue to help hold parts together.

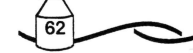

Ideas

- Use as many different shapes and textures as possible when putting together your sculpture.
- Make a mosaic out of small pieces of paper discarded from your trash aboard.
- Make a three-dimensional litter picture on construction paper using smaller pieces of litter.

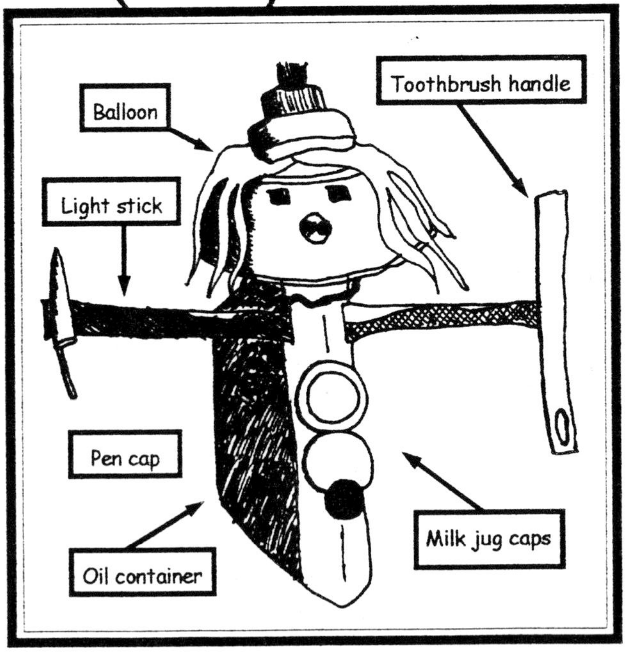

Self-portrait of a Boy

Make a Reusable Marked Line

Some of the activities in this book require a marked line to be used for towing or measuring depths. Make a marked line that can be shared amongst your research tools like the plankton net and secchi disk.

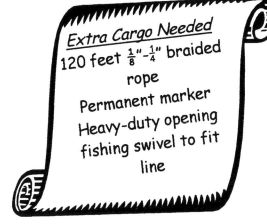

Extra Cargo Needed

120 feet $\frac{1}{8}$"-$\frac{1}{4}$" braided rope

Permanent marker

Heavy-duty opening fishing swivel to fit line

Getting Underway

Attach one of your swivels to one end of your rope with a secure knot.

Measuring from the swivel, mark your rope every meter (approx. 3.3 feet) or fathom (6 feet) any of the following ways:

- Use a permanent marker in a bright color.
- Tie knots.
- Sew colorful fabric strips in place.
- Thread colorful fabric strips through the rope and tie in place.

Since this rope will be used often with some of your tools from this book, you will want to make durable markings.

Using your Line

For each of your research tools like the secchi disk or plankton net, attach a short loop of rope to the towing place so that the swivel from your reusable rope can attach to it easily.

Now your long line can be attached and used with one tool then unattached and used with another. You now have one line for all your needs.

Just remember that your markings only go from the swivel along the rope. Remember to add the amount of space from the device to the swivel when taking length measurements.

Activities where you can use Your Line

- Make a Plankton Net page 41
- Make a Secchi Disk page 45
- Make your own Sounding Lead page 51

Make a Wind Generator

Learn what it takes to generate electricity with wind by making a wind generator from spare parts. Parental supervision is necessary during carving and around spinning fan blades.

Extra Cargo Needed

Thin wood scraps (Balsa wood is easily carved)
Small DC motor
Epoxy
Carving knife
(2) 1-2 ft. lengths of small wire with alligator clips on each end
Socket with small DC light bulb

You can also be a recycler and use the blade of an old fan if you find one.

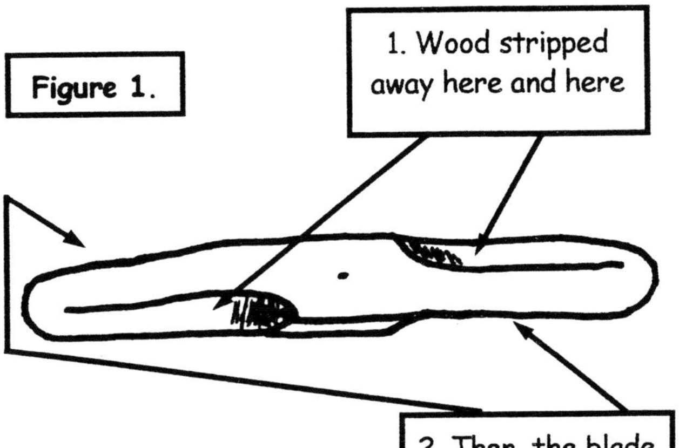

Getting Underway

Experiment with shaping your own wooden blade out of thin wood. Bevel the edges on each side of the wood to make the blade. When carving wood be careful to always take small shavings and cut away from you. See figure 1 for shaping ideas.

Drill a small hole in the center of your fan blade and position it onto the motor shaft so that it is a snug fit. Epoxy the blade into place. Let dry.

Clip each wire to one of the terminals on the motor. Now clip the wires to the lamp socket terminals. You're ready to see the wind light up your bulb. Take it out into a strong breeze and watch what happens.

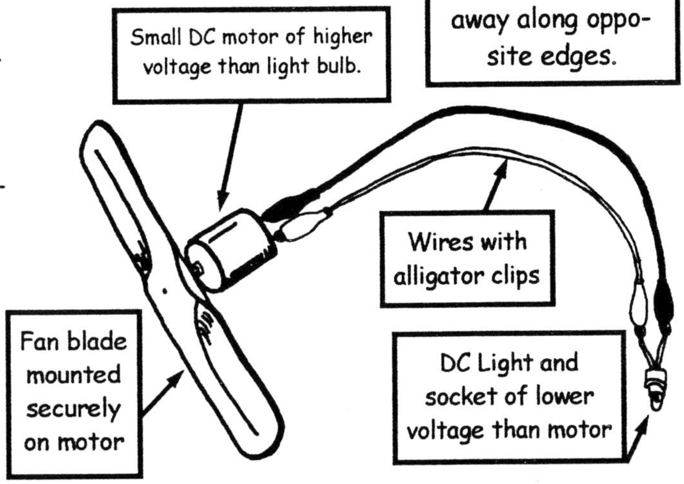

Take care when using sharp knives!
Be careful!
Spinning blades can hurt!

Alternate Course

Make a wind generator from a 12-volt fan by connecting the wires to a 3-6 volt lamp, and then test it in a strong breeze.

Sketch Journal

Interested in drawing? A sketch journal of your trip or your boating adventures is a wonderful ongoing activity.

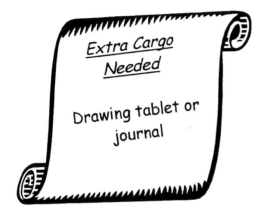

Extra Cargo Needed

Drawing tablet or journal

Ideas

- Have a family sketch journal where anyone can draw pictures of your boating adventures.
- Section areas of the sketch journal for different topics.
- Draw something from each trip or part of a trip.

A notebook with a hard back cover lets you do your drawing anywhere on the boat without the need for a table.

Getting Underway

Reserve a sketchpad or journal just for drawing while aboard your boat. There can be a theme to the sketch journal if you are particularly interested in drawing one type of subject like ocean animals, sea birds, landscapes, boats, etc. Or, just draw what is on your mind. Bring the sketch journal whenever you go boating. Being on a boat gives you a special viewpoint for your sketching.

Make your sketch journal as special as you are!

The Hunt is On!

Make your next boating trip into a huge scavenger hunt. If other boats are traveling with you, get them to play as well.

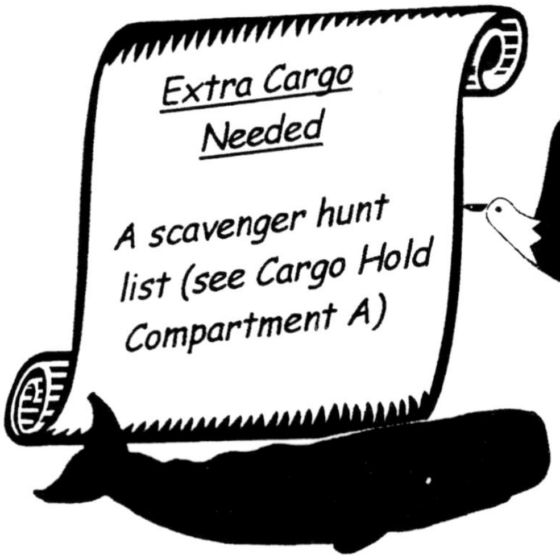
Extra Cargo Needed
A scavenger hunt list (see Cargo Hold Compartment A)

Getting Underway

Before leaving on a boat trip, make up a scavenger hunt list or use one of the examples provided in Compartment A of the Cargo Hold. There's even a blank one you can customize.

If you'll be traveling with other boats, ask them if they would like to join in on the fun.

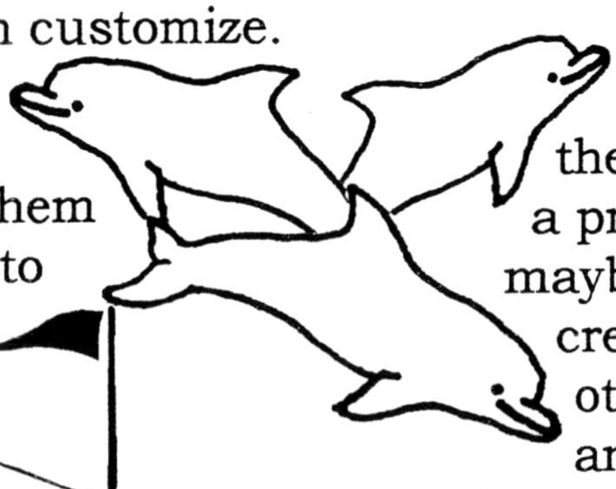

Items on your list should be something you may see on your trip. Each sighting is worth 10 points. You can limit the score by having one sighting of each item allowed per day if your trip will last more than one day.

The items must be seen by at least two people in order for it to count. See how many points you can get. Try to earn a certain amount by the end of the passage to win a prize for the whole family--maybe dinner ashore or ice cream. Or compete with the other boats that want to play and decide on a prize with them. If you are playing with other boats, it's fun to check-in daily with your score.

A Learning Day Trip

Take a day off from your normal boating routine and go for a learning day trip. Everyone can brush up on their seamanship skills as you experiment along the way.

Getting Underway

Parents, this is a day of experimentation and exploration; don't plan to go anywhere in particular. Find out "what happens if… when you do this." It will increase everyone's boating skills at a time when it doesn't matter if you are off course.

As your kids learn to operate and maneuver the family's boat, it will increase their sense of pride, teach them about the responsibility of boat ownership, and foster an interest in taking care of the boat. Ideas for making the most of this learning day trip are included, but don't hesitate to come up with more of your own!

Ideas for All Boats with Motors

- At anchor or at the dock, go through the steps of starting your boat's engine then have the kids try. Someone can even make a checklist.
- Younger kids have a great time learning how responsive your steering is. Have them find out how tight of a circle the boat can turn.
- In open waters, older kids can try tricky maneuvers using reverse at slow speeds.
- If a buoy is nearby, use it to maneuver next to and around.
- As the kids get better at steering, throw a boat cushion out and have the crew try to retrieve it without the captain's help.

Ideas for Sailboats

- Experiment with different sail arrangements.
- With just the mainsail up, have the kids turn the boat in a full circle so they can see how the wind fills and changes the sail through the turn.
- Let your kids put your boat in irons then have them try to get the boat going again.
- Try to backwind the boat with only the foresail up and having it sheeted on the windward side. Can you sail it backwards?
- Practice heaving-to. Come about without releasing the jib sheet. Then tie your tiller or wheel so that it steers you about 60° into the wind. You can add a double or triple-reefed mainsail or a trysail (if you have it) sheeted flat. Throw something small and biodegradable overboard to see if you are moving. Some boats heave-to better than others. Does yours do better with or without the mainsail?
- As your crew advances in their seamanship skills, use your motor less and less until you can sail in and out of anchorages or docks.

More Ideas for Boats with Motors

- In a shallow area, practice maneuvering the boat by kedging with an anchor. Carefully toss an anchor and line out and pull yourself and the boat as you haul in the anchor. Make sure the bitter end is tied off! This is a skill that may be required if caught in tight corners without your engine.
- Heave-to under power by steering the boat into the wind or a few degrees off the wind with only enough power to have steerage.
- If you are staying at a dock, teach the kids how to dock the boat when you return.

Object Overboard

During one of your boating trips, throw a brightly colored floatable object overboard and try to retrieve it.

Getting Underway

Position one person at the bow of the boat with a brightly colored boat cushion and another person with the watch. Using a cushion with a handle will help you retrieve it. Have a boat hook and long handled net ready. The person that throws is the one to watch the cushion and give directions to the helmsman. That person never takes his/her eyes off of the cushion. The timekeeper also relays directions if the helmsman can't hear the spotter. Use hand signals to insure that everyone understands. But, the spotter should decide whether to point in the direction he/she wants the helmsman to steer or to point to the overboard item. Explain your hand signals before the activity so that the person steering understands.

As you near the object motion to the helmsman to slow down. It is important to be going slow as you attempt to retrieve an object. If it is windy, maneuver around the object and bring the boat into the wind. Then the object will be floating towards you. As you scoop up the object, yell to the timekeeper to check the time.

Do this activity several times until you and the rest of the crew become a real team and you improve your time.

This activity is great practice for retrieving mooring rings, hats, cushions, and even people.

Ready, Set, GO!

Ideas

- ☞ If you have a sailboat, try retrieving your float under sail.
- ☞ Retrieve a half-filled jug of water for a real challenge.
- ☞ Take turns being the person that keeps his eyes on the float and the one who steers.
- ☞ Do this activity in all kinds of weather.

Alternate Courses

- ☸ Do a crewperson overboard drill sometime when the water is warm and safe.
- ☸ If the water is cool, put one of your crew overboard in a dinghy to wait to be rescued.

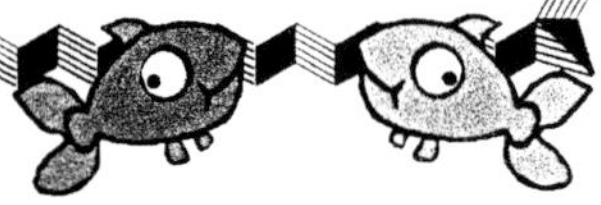

Object Overboard Time Sheet				
Date	**Object**	**Beg. Time**	**End. Time**	**Total Time**

Dinghy Fun

Do you have a dinghy? When the wind is right, set up a buoyed sailing, motoring, or rowing course (away from any channels) and go out for a dinghy ride.

Remember to wear your life jackets!
Extra Cargo Needed
Dinghy
Quiet harbor
Milk jugs

Getting Underway

Set up a course with buoys (if there are no buoys already existing, use sealed plastic milk jugs tied to an anchor or other weight) and practice with your inflatable, sailing, or rowing dinghy. Try to round the buoys as closely as possible without touching them. Let everyone practice his or her maneuvering skills.

Ideas

- If there are others in the area with dinghies, set up a friendly race.
- In a quiet harbor, blindfold your helmsman and have another person try to give directions back to the mother ship.

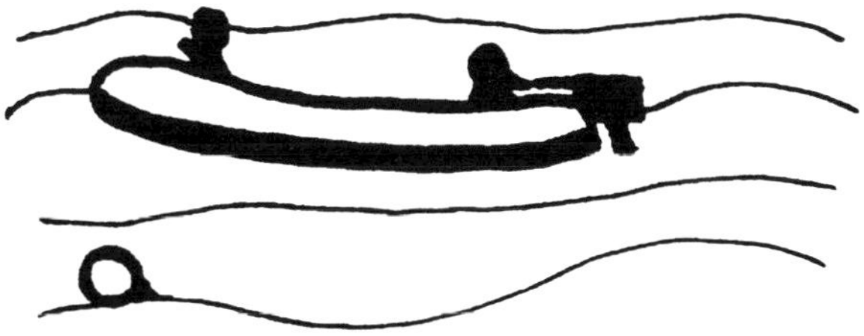

Shaving Cream Fun

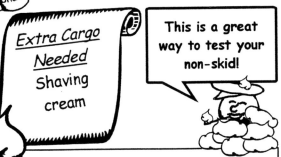

Shaving cream isn't just for shaving! Get an extra can for foamy fun in the cockpit.

Extra Cargo Needed
Shaving cream

This is a great way to test your non-skid!

Do not get shaving cream in your eyes. Brands that contain menthol can burn in particular! Also DO NOT put it in your mouth or ingest it!

Getting Underway

The decks of a boat are the ultimate arena for messy play. Clean up is a breeze with water and a bucket.

Don your swimsuits, close the companionway and hatches, and open your hands for a big foamy fistful of shaving cream. Dress your face up like Santa, experiment with foamy hairdos, cover yourself in foam, or throw it around. Have some good clean foamy fun! But, be careful not to get it in your eyes. And try not to slip too much or at least not too quickly!

When it's clean up time, just bucket yourself and the cockpit. Then you can shower off when you have fresh water available. You and the boat will be smelling fresh for days! It may even get up some of those scuff marks!

Whip cream can be used also but it does not work as well. The high percentage of fat in the foam makes cleanup harder, requiring several washings with soap and water. And, since it has a great deal of sugar in it as well, it feels pretty sticky until clean up time.

Alternate Course

Shaving cream makes a wonderful medium for finger painting for young kids that no longer put things in their mouths. Spray a little on a dark colored cookie sheet or broiler pan for them to draw and experiment with their fingers.

Make a Kamal

Ancient Arabic mariners relied on the kamal for navigation. (Pronounced kuh-mawl) Now you can make your own version of a kamal.

Extra Cargo Needed

Stiff plastic sheeting or cardboard
String
Metric ruler
Craft Knife

The material you use for your kamal needs to be stiff enough so that it won't bend when held by the two points of the bridle.

Getting Underway

Cut a piece of stiff cardboard or plastic 15 centimeters long and 4 centimeters wide.

Along one long edge of the card, mark the card every centimeter. Poke a hole in the middle of the card 2 centimeters in from each short side.

Cut a piece of string 20 centimeters long and thread each end into one of the holes of the card and knot the ends to make a bridle.

Draw up the bridle between two fingers and attach another piece of string about 60 centimeters long.

With a ruler and with the card on its edge, measure 57 centimeters from the card along the string attached to the bridle. Tie a knot at this 57-centimeter mark.

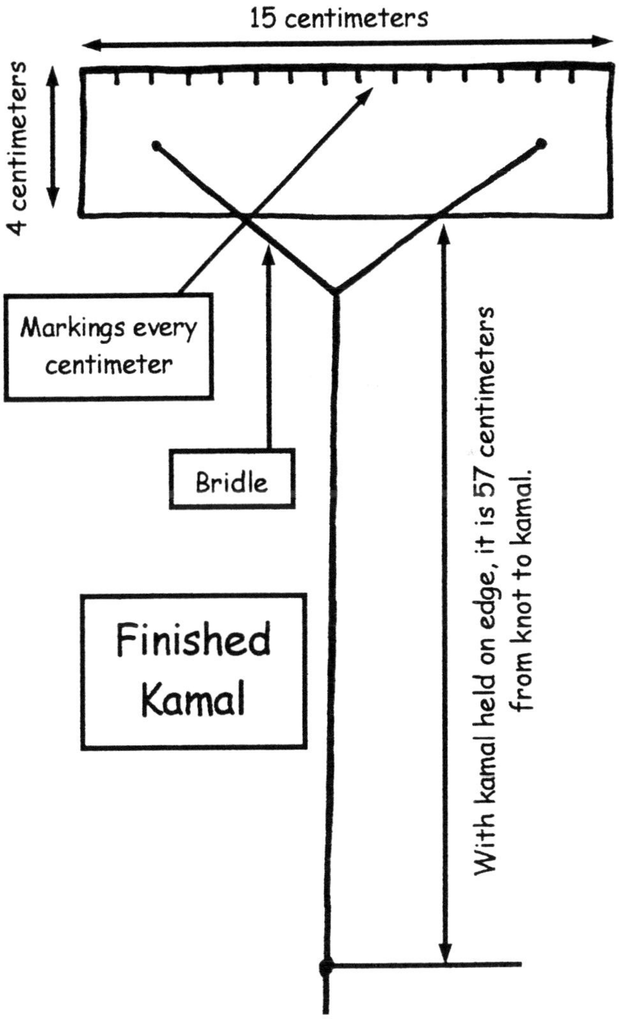

Using your Kamal

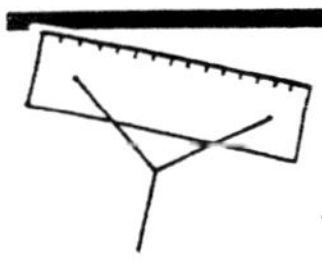

Learn to use your kamal to find distances from charted landforms or navigation aids.

Extra Cargo Needed
Kamal from previous page
Kamals are particularly accurate for measuring small angles of less than 15° or so.

Getting Underway

Your kamal is calibrated so that each centimeter is one degree of measurement. Your eyes need to remain 57 centimeters from the kamal to take an accurate sighting. The knot and line help you keep that distance. Hold the knot in your teeth while keeping the card in front of you with the string taut. Steady yourself with your other hand. Some people with short arms may not be able to take as accurate of a sighting with the kamal if the string is not taut when the knot is held between their teeth.

Kamals can be used to measure angles of width and height. Holding the kamal horizontally will measure angles of width. And, holding your kamal vertically will measure angles of height or altitude.

Ideas on Using your Kamal

- Measure the angle between two charted points that you can see. You could measure the angle between two edges of a charted island. See example on page 75.
- You can also measure vertically. Measuring angles of altitude require you to be pretty close to the object, about 3 miles or within view of the true shoreline where you are measuring. As an example you could measure the number of degrees from the bottom of a lighthouse to the top. See example on page 76.

Indian and Arabic explorers used kamals as they navigated their dhows in the Persian Gulf and Red Sea.

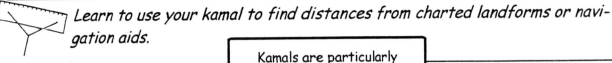

Example 1: Finding your Distance to an Object

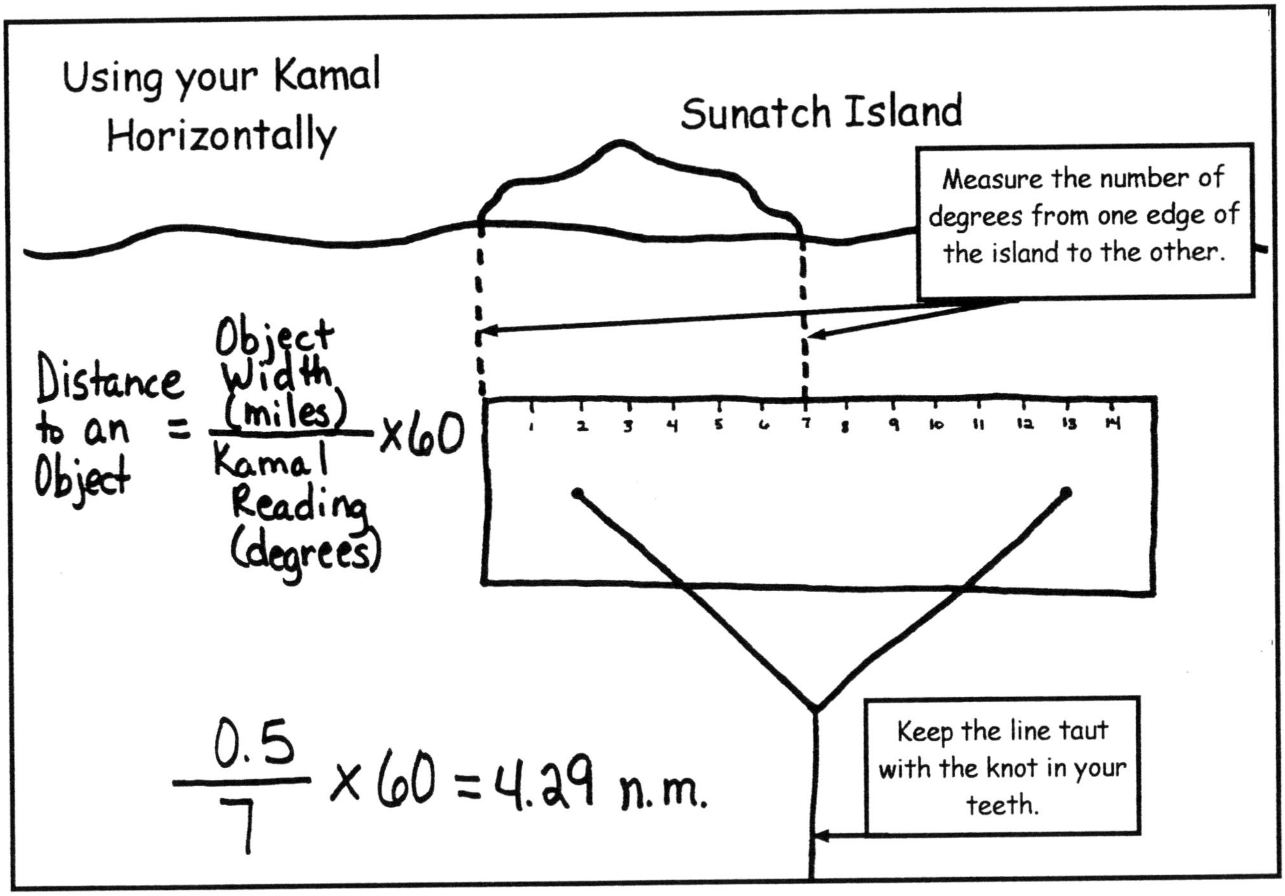

To find the distance away from an object, divide the known width of the object by the kamal reading in degrees then multiply by 60.

While boating, you see an island in the distance. Knowing where you are, you see on your chart that it is Sunatch Island. With your dividers calibrated with the chart's scale, you measure how wide Sunatch Island is at the edges you viewed on deck. You find that it is .5 nautical miles across from the direction you are approaching.

With your kamal, you go back on deck and sight the one edge of your kamal to one side of the island and count the number of degrees it is to the other side of the island. You count 7° degrees.

Using the formula in the picture above you calculate that it is 4.29 miles away.

Example 2: Finding your Distance to an Object

While sailing, you see that you are approaching Sunatch Point Light and wonder how far away you are. According to the Light List, you find that it is 120 feet above sea level. Armed with your kamal, you go on deck and line up the upper edge of your kamal vertically with the light of the light house. Your thumb marks where the edge of land meets sea level. You know that you are fairly close to shore because you can see the true shore line and there is not much tide range in this area.

To find the distance away from an object, divide the height of the object by the kamal angle multiplied by 100.

It is 4° degrees from shoreline to top of light house. Using the formula below you find that you are 0.3 miles away.

USEFUL FORMULAS FOR THE KAMAL

Distance away = Object Width (feet) ÷ 100 x Kamal Angle (degrees)

Distance away = { Object Width (miles) ÷ Kamal Angle (degrees) } x 60

Distance away = Object Height (feet) ÷ 100 x Kamal Angle (degrees) Within view of true shoreline

Your thumb marks the shoreline edge

$$\frac{120}{100 \times 4} = 0.3 \text{ nautical miles away}$$

Using your Kamal Vertically

$$\text{Distance to an Object} = \frac{\text{Height of Object (feet)}}{100 \times \text{Kamal Reading (degrees)}}$$

Keep line taut with knot in teeth

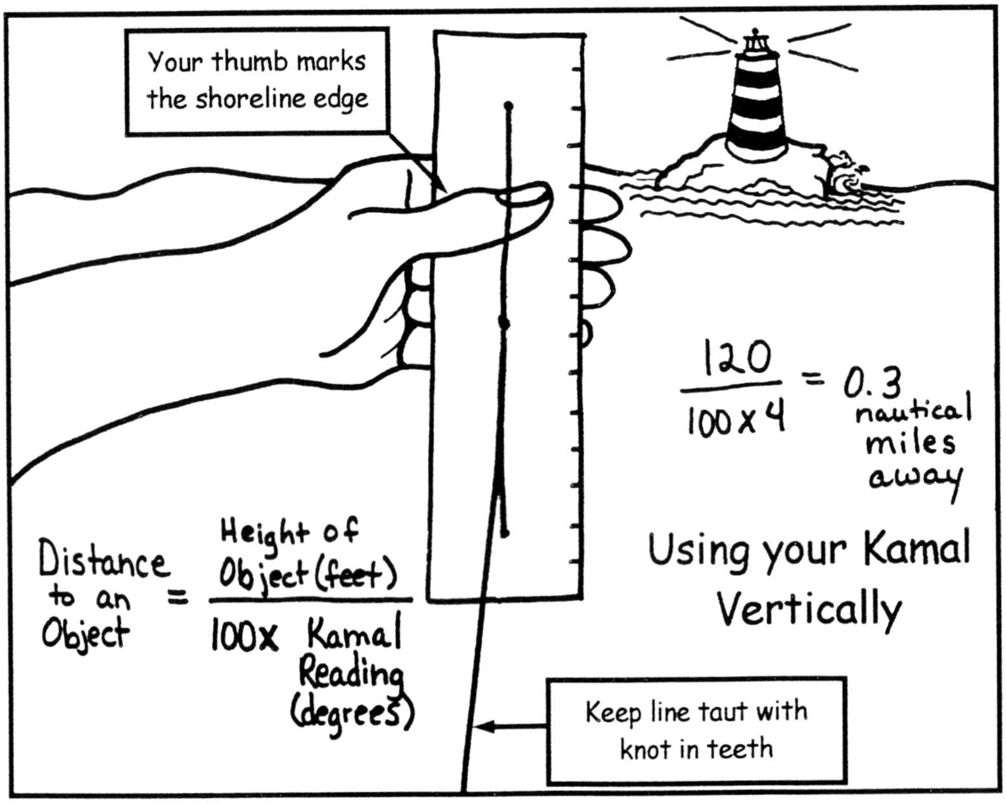

Make a Hydrometer

Hydrometers are used by oceanographers and marine biologists to test the density of sea water samples. You can make your own hydrometer and measure the change in density of the waters you travel through.

Extra Cargo Needed
2 non-clicky ball point pens
Small crimp-on lead fishing weights
Pliers
Bucket and water
It's important to use 2 of the same brand pens.
Use only ball point pens that have no small hole in the casing. Bic brand Round Stic® pens work well.

Getting Underway

With your pliers, remove the ball point and ink cartridge of the pen from the casing. Be careful not to smash the ink cartridge or you will have ink dripping on everything! See figure 1.

Add the small lead weights to the casing only until it will float upright without tipping over. The number is dependent on the size of the weights being used and the size of the casing. See figure 2.

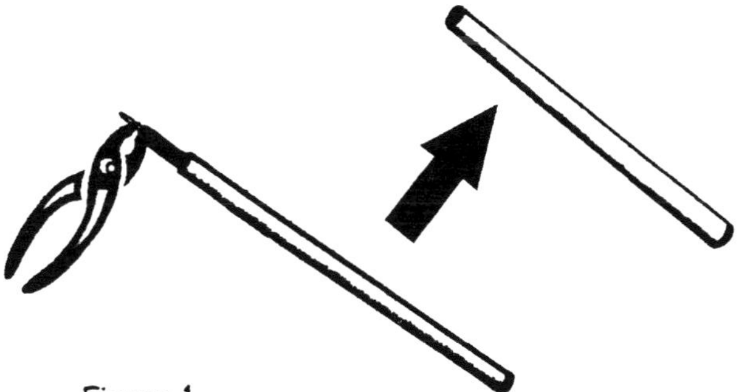

Figure 1.

Make sure that the bottom plug on the casing is tight.

Float this empty casing in the bucket of water holding it from falling over into the water.

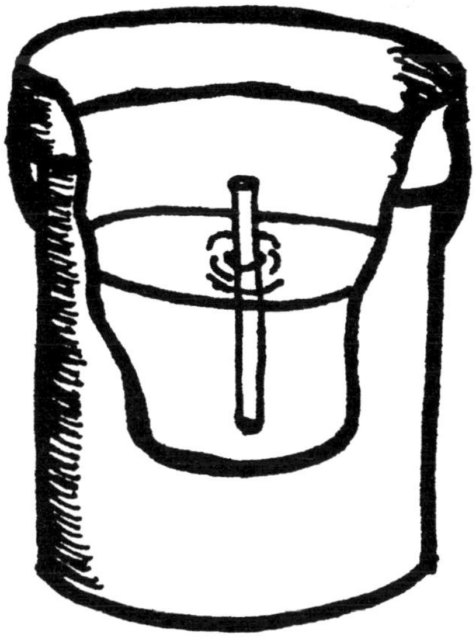

Figure 2.

Finishing your Hydrometer

If the inside of your casing is wet, use a twisted paper towel or cotton swab to dry the inside.

Remove the bottom plug from the second pen and place in the top of your hydrometer to keep the weights from falling out in storage. See figure 3. Your hydrometer is finished!

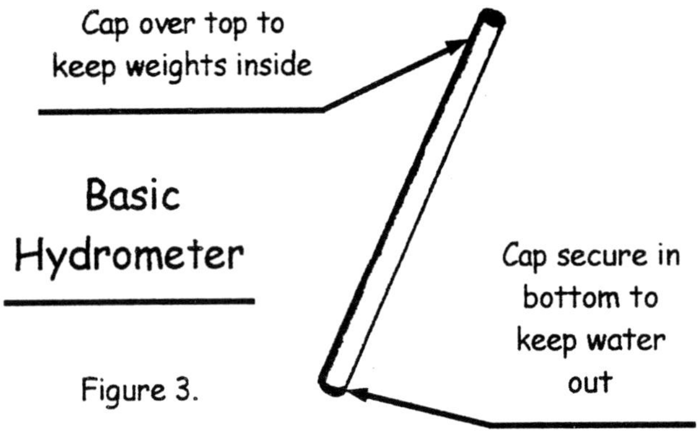

Figure 3.

Calibrating your Hydrometer

In order to calibrate your hydrometer, you will need some distilled water.

Float your hydrometer in a full tall glass of distilled water. Mark your hydrometer at the exact level that the top of the water touches the hydrometer. Take your hydrometer out of the water and dry it off. Draw a line completely around the hydrometer at that level. Use a permanent marker.➚

Never leave your hydrometer in liquid for long. While the caps do keep water out, they are not infallible and will begin to leak in time. If your hydrometer begins taking in water, the readings will not be reliable. Time to make a new one!

Alternate Courses

- Use your calibrated hydrometer to measure the density of the water whenever you sight whales or dolphins.
- Use your hydrometer to measure the density of the water whenever a fish is caught.
- Use your hydrometer at every anchorage or marina stop and see how the density changes as you travel.

Now carefully mark your hydrometer every centimeter from that line both above and below using a metric ruler. Distilled water has a density of 10 so mark your line that goes all the way around with the number 10. The marks above that line get numbers descending from 10 (for less dense liquids) and below the 10 have increasing numbers (for more dense liquids).

Now test your hydrometer in salt water, milk, vinegar, any liquids. Watch how the level where it floats changes! While it isn't as exact as a professional hydrometer it will give you a good idea of how the density of the water changes as you travel to other places.

Calibrated Hydrometer

Poetry in Motion

The movement of a boat through the water is the inspiration for many poems. Create your own as you listen to how your boat responds to wind and waves.

Getting Underway

This is the perfect activity for a lazy day or evening when the only noise is your boat moving through the water. Close your eyes and clear your mind of all ideas.

Picture your boat as she moves through the water. Think of descriptive words and phrases that illustrate what your mind is seeing.

Now open your eyes and write those ideas down. What did you hear, feel, smell? What do you see now that your eyes are open? Put together phrases and statements from the words and ideas you have conjured and you have a poem.

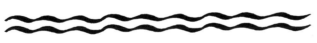

Ideas

- ✍ Do the same for your boat at anchor or at the dock.
- ✍ You could even create a poem about your dinghy.

Sailing the Banshee

By Amie Fort

Push off from the beach
Raise up the sail
And point the tiller
We're Off!
We speed along,
pass up the island
and run with the dolphins,
Heeling from the wind.

Uh Oh! Getting rough!
We flip over!
Stand on the keel,
And right her!

PHEW! We sail back to rest.

Seaweed Art

If your boating takes you into areas abundant in floating seaweed, gather some and create your own seaweed art! Seaweed mountings make beautiful collectibles, even holiday cards.

Extra Cargo Needed
- Seaweed
- Heavy paper
- Bucket or basin

> Seaweed that is very thick or stiff may not work well for this activity

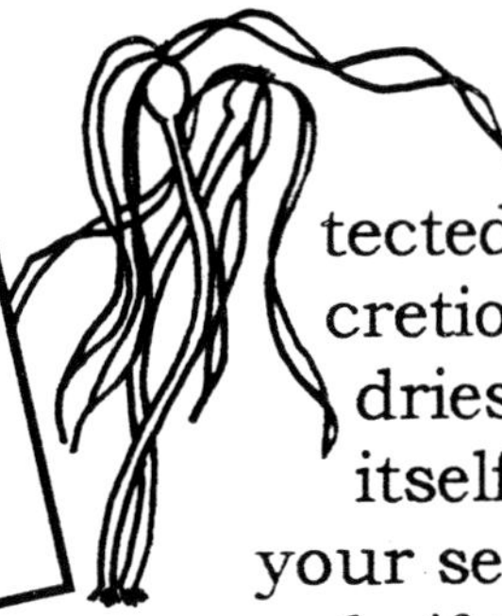

Getting Underway

Carefully gather fresh seaweed with a net as you travel.

Float a manageable sized piece of seaweed in a basin of water. Trim the seaweed with your scissors if it is too large or if it has too many overlapping branches. The size and shape will depend on the size of the paper and whether you will turn it into a card.

Slide a piece of heavy paper underneath the seaweed. As you get closer to the seaweed with your paper, arrange the seaweed in a pleasing shape.

Gently remove the paper from the water. Be careful to keep the seaweed arranged on the paper.

> If you trim the seaweed with scissors, remember to rinse them in fresh water when finished.

Let the seaweed and paper sit in the sun protected from any wind. The secretions of the seaweed as it dries will act as a glue to bind itself to the paper. Identify your seaweed. Collect samples only if there is an abundance of the same variety in that area.

Happy Holidays
From the Ocean!

Storing your Creations

After the seaweed is partially dried, cover it with a sheet of wax paper, then press between newspapers and large books until completely dried. Well, at least until as dry as it will get aboard a boat!

Some seaweeds will need to be glued to the mounting paper after being completely dried.

Drawing Contour Lines

Here is a fun activity about drawing the contour lines of a rock to help you understand how contour lines are drawn on charts and maps.

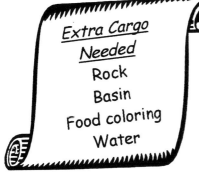

Extra Cargo Needed

Rock
Basin
Food coloring
Water

Getting Underway

While ashore sometime, find an interesting rock to bring back to the boat. This will become a small island that you will draw contour lines for just like a real contour-lined chart.

On a calm day back at the boat, decide how the island will sit in your pretend ocean, your basin of water. Place your dry rock directly on your paper as it will sit in the ocean and trace its outer most edge onto the paper.

Now position your island in the middle of your basin and fill it with 1" of water. It may help to add food coloring to the water. Looking directly above your ocean and straight down onto your island, notice the next contour line of the island at the water line.

Contour lines drawn very close together mean that the topography of the land is very steep. As lines get farther apart, the land becomes less steep. Places without lines show flat areas. Think about this as you attempt to draw contour lines for your little island.

Draw it on your paper trying to be as accurate as possible. Since your base line is the outer most edge of your "island", any subsequent lines should be inside the first line.

Add another inch of water and draw the next contour line where the water line touches your island rock.

Continue adding water an inch at a time, drawing the remaining contour lines until the island rock is completely submerged. See examples on the following page.

Congratulations! You've made your own island chart! You can also add a drawing of a lighthouse or your boat traveling nearby.

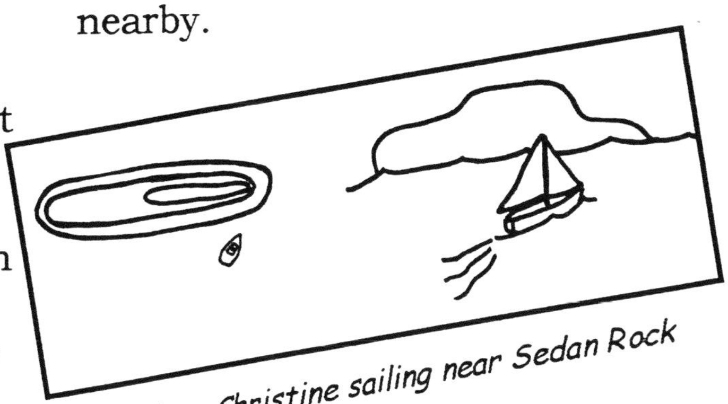

Lindsay Christine sailing near Sedan Rock

Each line = an elevation increase of 1 inch.

Figure 1. Chicken Leg Rock

In the example at left of Chicken Leg Rock, there are few contour lines. Since the island levels off after the first steep increase in elevation, only a few contour lines are required.

In the example at right, you can see that Mashed Potato Rock has contour lines that show how the rock gradually gets smaller and taller like a dollop of mashed potatoes.

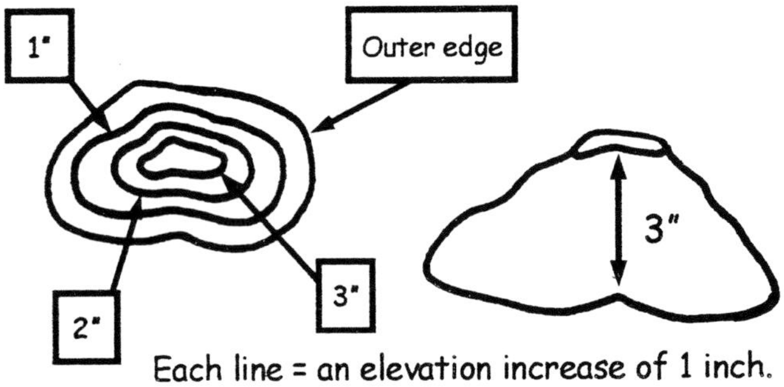

Each line = an elevation increase of 1 inch.

Figure 2. Mashed Potato Rock

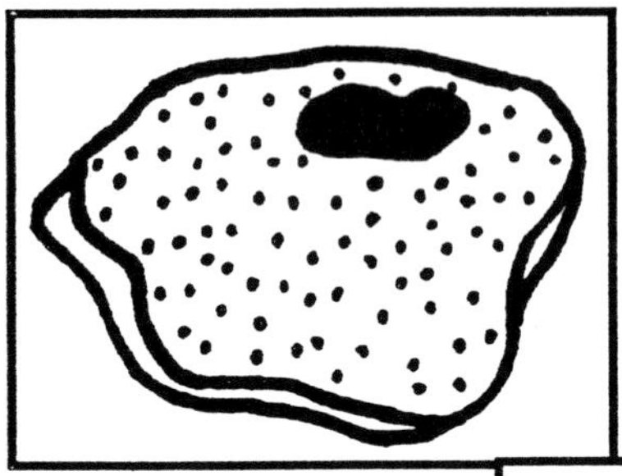

In order to show the levels better, we shaded in the areas.

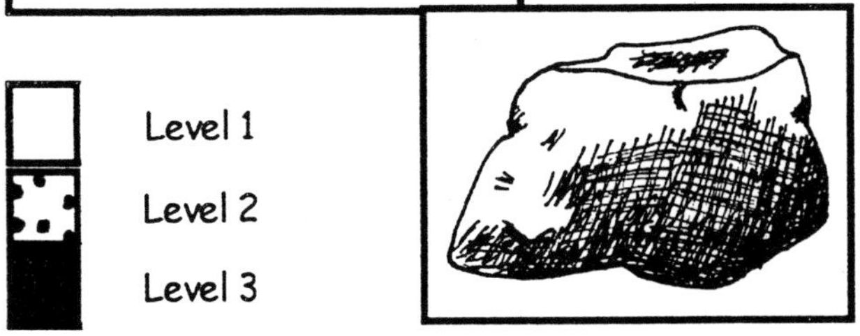

Figure 3.

The space between contour lines is dependent on the size of the rock or item you choose. Smaller rocks could have contour lines drawn every $\frac{1}{4}$" or $\frac{1}{2}$" of water height.

Alternate Courses

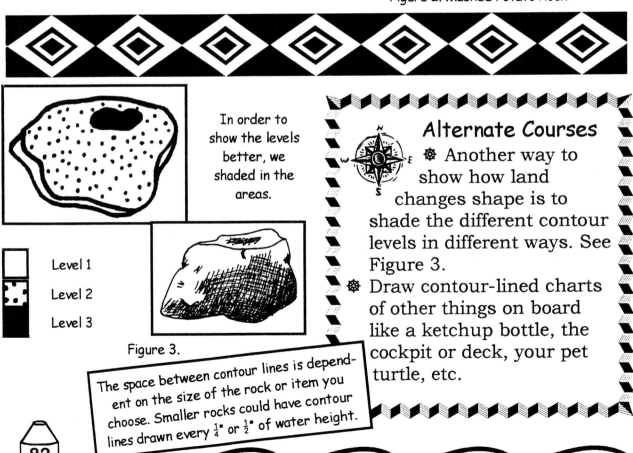

- Another way to show how land changes shape is to shade the different contour levels in different ways. See Figure 3.
- Draw contour-lined charts of other things on board like a ketchup bottle, the cockpit or deck, your pet turtle, etc.

Make a Personal Reading Light

Learn about electricity. Make a personal reading light that can be run for hours with negligible power usage. Parental supervision is suggested when working with soldering iron.

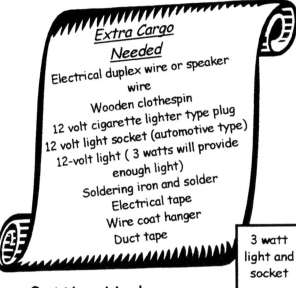

Extra Cargo Needed

Electrical duplex wire or speaker wire
Wooden clothespin
12 volt cigarette lighter type plug
12 volt light socket (automotive type)
12-volt light (3 watts will provide enough light)
Soldering iron and solder
Electrical tape
Wire coat hanger
Duct tape

Getting Underway

Cut enough electrical wire to go from the place where it will be used to the closest outlet. Separate about one inch of the electrical wire and strip off 1/8 inch of the insulation from the ends of each wire.

Solder each wire to one of the two terminals of the light socket. Polarity is not important. Tape the connections so that the two bare wires cannot come into contact with each other. See figure 1.

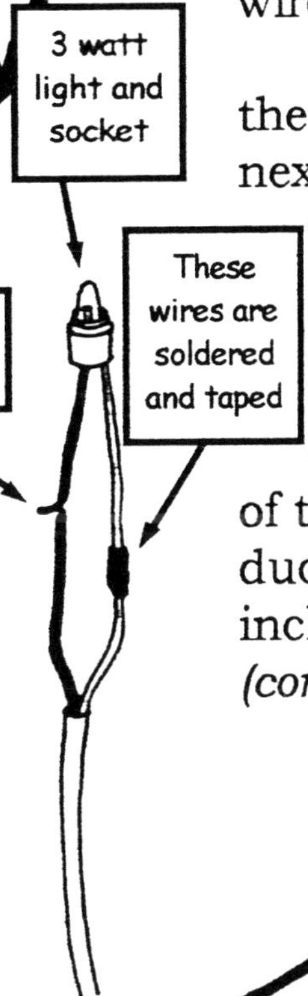

Figure 1.

Cut a piece of the coat hanger about 8 inches long. Wrap electrical tape around the first inch of the stiff wire.

Place the socket next to the piece of stiff wire where the electrical tape is and with duct tape, tape them together. Place the electrical wire along the rest of the stiff wire and wrap with duct tape leaving the last two inches untaped for now.

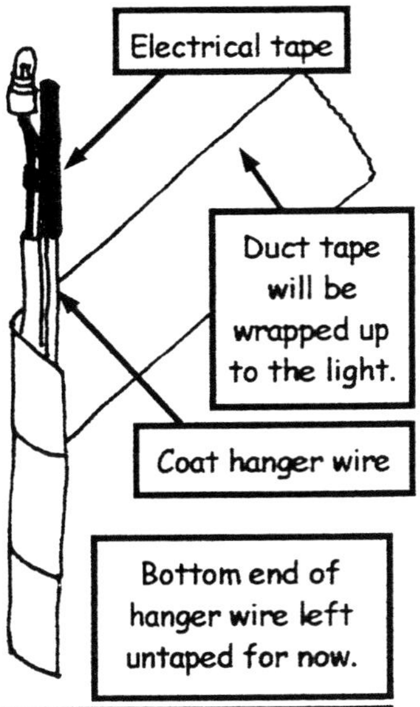

Figure 2.

(continued)

Getting Underway (Continued)

Bend the end of the stiff wire with the socket attached into a hook shape, then attach one clothes pin "handle" or side along the inside of the hook. The placement of the clothespin is dependent upon where you would like the light to be when you clip it to a book for reading. Tape the handle firmly with duct tape. See figure 3.

Solder and tape the remaining ends of the electrical wire to the 12-volt plug. Now you have a reading light that can be clipped almost anywhere. For safety, make sure that your 12-volt receptacle is properly fused.

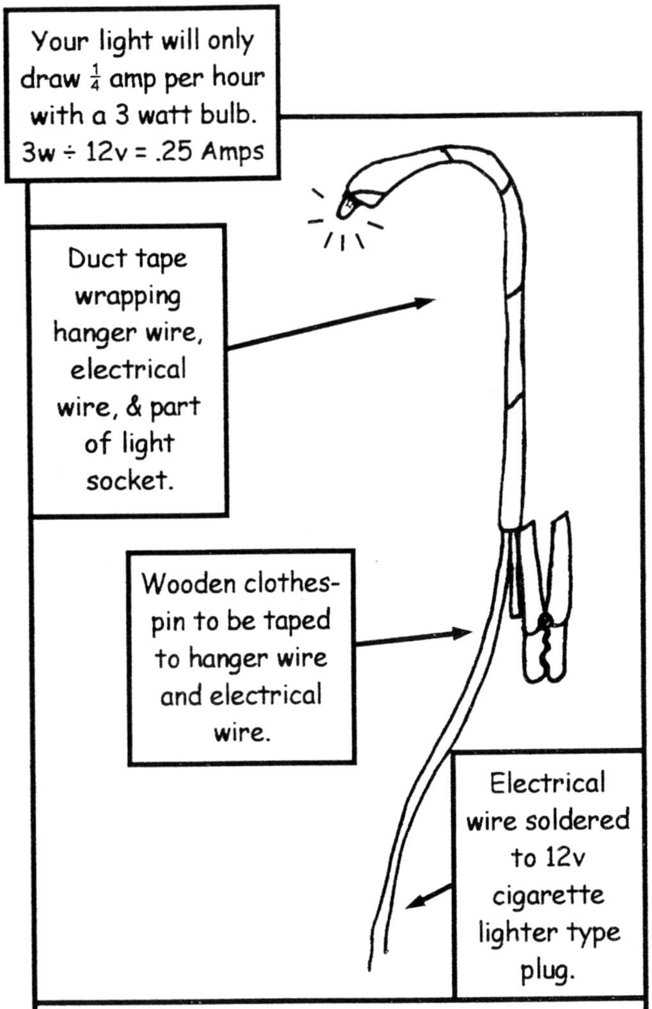
Your light will only draw $\frac{1}{4}$ amp per hour with a 3 watt bulb. 3w ÷ 12v = .25 Amps
Duct tape wrapping hanger wire, electrical wire, & part of light socket.
Wooden clothespin to be taped to hanger wire and electrical wire.
Electrical wire soldered to 12v cigarette lighter type plug.
Figure 3.

DC stands for direct current. It is an electric current that flows in one direction only. Most boat systems operate away from shore on DC power.
AC stands for alternating current. It is an electric current that continually reverses its direction of flow. Shore power is an example of AC power.
A lightning bolt produces 100 million volts!

Anchorage Journal

Record information about each anchorage you visit aboard your boat. Along with helping you remember all the fun you've had exploring, it may be helpful to your family and others who may want to visit those places in the future.

Getting Underway

Look in Compartment A of the Cargo Hold for anchorage journal log sheets you can photocopy and use. Or, see page 171 to order our Marina/Anchorage Journal.

Include information you would want to have if you were planning a visit for the first time.

The more information included in your log, the more helpful it will be in the future.

If you like to draw, include a drawing of the anchorage or view from your boat at each location.

Ideas

- 🕮 Record the name of the anchorage.
- 🕮 Document the location of anchorage general directions, closest city and maybe GPS waypoints.
- 🕮 List the dates you were anchored.
- 🕮 Write in the number of boats anchored with your boat.
- 🕮 Record notable hazards inside anchorage and on the approach.
- 🕮 Make note of interesting things found on shore.
- 🕮 List tips for returning.
- 🕮 Document the depth your boat anchored in.
- 🕮 Write in the type of bottom and holding.
- 🕮 Include the weather you encountered.
- 🕮 Explain the prevailing wind for that time of year.
- 🕮 Record the protection from the wind and swell.
- 🕮 Decide what overall grade or rating from 1-10 each anchorage should get.

Clean up an Oil Spill

Using the supplies listed below, try to keep an oil spill away from your little boat or sea creature and then try to clean it up!

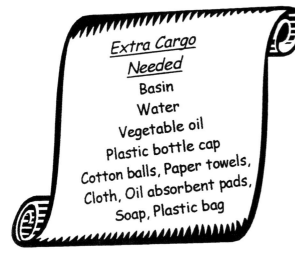

Extra Cargo Needed

Basin
Water
Vegetable oil
Plastic bottle cap
Cotton balls, Paper towels,
Cloth, Oil absorbent pads,
Soap, Plastic bag

Getting Underway

Fill your basin $\frac{1}{3}$ full with water, and float your plastic bottle cap in it. This cap is your little ship or sea animal that you will try to protect from the oil spill.

Add two tablespoons of vegetable oil to the basin.

Just like a large oil spill in the ocean, the oil in your basin will break up with movement of the water. Try to protect your little boat from the oil spill. Use pieces of a plastic shopping bag (the handles work well as containment fenders), paper towel, cloth, etc. to keep the oil away from the boat. Then try to clean up your oil spill. Try each item listed and see which one works best.

Ideas

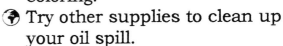

- To make your basin of water look more like the ocean, try adding a few drops of blue food coloring.
- Try other supplies to clean up your oil spill.
- Use a little rubber duck as your animal in peril. How can you clean him up so that he can survive?
- Use salt water in your miniature ocean. Does the oil act any differently? Is it harder or easier to clean up?
- Come up with a clean-up plan if your boat were to spill fuel or oil into the water.
- What happens when you add detergent?

See if you can protect your little boat from the oil spill and get it cleaned up before it gets to her.

Make your own Compass

By magnetizing a steel needle, you can make your own compass and find out where North and South are.

WATCH OUT! Remember to keep all magnets away from your ship's compass at all times so that it will not influence the compass reading.

Extra Cargo Needed

- Magnet
- Steel needle
- Slice of cork or styrofoam
- Tape
- Small bowl of water

Be careful not to use too big of a piece of Styrofoam or cork. It will make it too hard for the needle to turn it.

The earth's magnetic field is believed to be caused by currents of electrically charged particles in the liquid iron outer core of the earth.

Getting Underway

To magnetize your needle, draw the needle along the magnet repeatedly for about five minutes. Rotate the needle periodically so that all surfaces make contact with the magnet. By always drawing your needle across the magnet in the same direction, you will be magnetizing the needle by aligning the domains in the steel to all point in a North/ South direction.

Tape your needle to the slice of cork or Styrofoam and float it in your bowl of water. The North seeking pole of the needle will turn to point to the magnetic North Pole.

Huangdi, the Yellow Emporer of China, ruled from 2697-2597 B.C. He is known for inventing the compass.

To make it easier for your compass to turn, break the surface tension of the water with a small drop of liquid soap.

Compass in a bowl

Create a Fishing Log

Chronicle your catches so you can remember that big fish and even the little ones you catch as you boat.

Extra Cargo Needed
Photocopies of Fishing Log from Compartment A of the Cargo Hold.

Getting Underway

Create a fishing log to document where and when you have been successful or unsuccessful fishing. Record what bait was used, the times, weather, etc.

Pick from the different fishing log pages available to you in Compartment A of the Cargo Hold to photocopy. Or, see page 171 to order our Fishing Log. Each time you fish, write down whatever information you think may be helpful for you to track.

Later, go back to the places where you caught fish and try to recreate the time by looking in your logbook. Do you catch fish again?

Ideas

- Record the water's density every time you fish with your hydrometer from page 77.
- Log the size, type, and weight of each fish caught.
- After logging each catch, record the weather and sea state.
- Jot down the kind of baits or lures you tried each time you fish whether successful or not.
- Troll your plankton net from page 41 for a few seconds while fishing. Document what you find.
- Find the clarity of the water by using your secchi disk from page 45.

Ship Watching

A great hobby to pick up while you are boating is ship watching. You can learn quite a bit about a ship when you know what to look for when watching them.

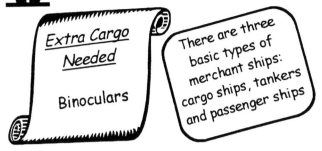

Extra Cargo Needed

Binoculars

There are three basic types of merchant ships: cargo ships, tankers and passenger ships

Getting Underway

If you boat in an area that has any shipping traffic, start watching ships. Try to identify the type of ship by its shape. By the lines on the stern and bow, you can find out if it is full of cargo or empty and ready for cargo.

Here is some basic information to help you with your ship watching.

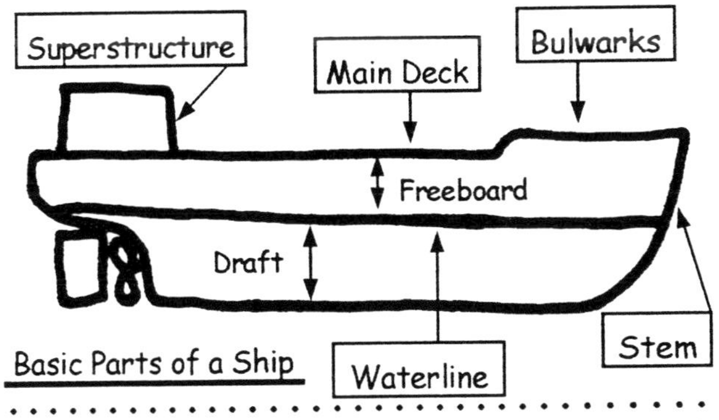

Basic Parts of a Ship

Roll-on/Roll-off ships have large openings in the stern or side of the hull so that cargo can be rolled aboard. These cargo ships carry cars, trucks, and other rolled aboard cargo.

Ideas

- Make note of names of ships and where they are from. You may end up seeing them over and over. (See the Flag Journal activity for more ideas).
- See if the funnel is painted to show the name of the shipping line or the country of the vessel.
- Look for the draft markings and plimsoll lines telling you how full the ship is and how deep its draft is.

Tanker showing separate tanks and bulkheads. The largest can hold 500,000 short tons of oil.

Container Ship with containers shown. The largest of these can carry up to 1000 containers.

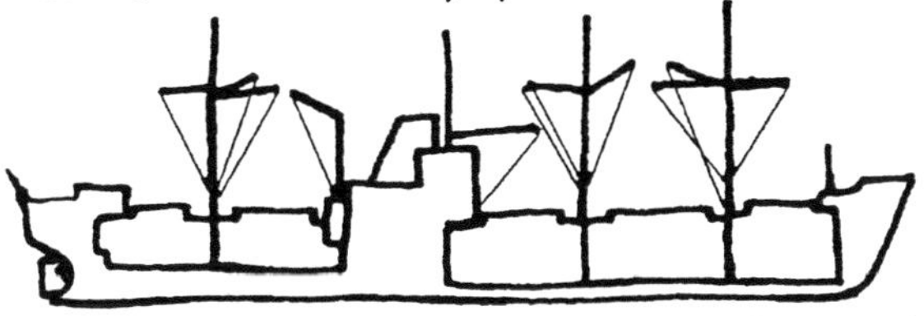

General Cargo Ship showing cargo holds. It takes container and cargo ships about 21 days to go round trip from the US to Europe.

Basic Ship Markings

International Load-Lines

The International Load-Line Convention regulates ship loading according to the size, type of cargo, and route of the vessel. These Load-Line marks are painted at the midpoint of the vessel port and starboard and help to balance the ship as well as insure the vessel is not overloaded.

Great Lakes Load-Lines

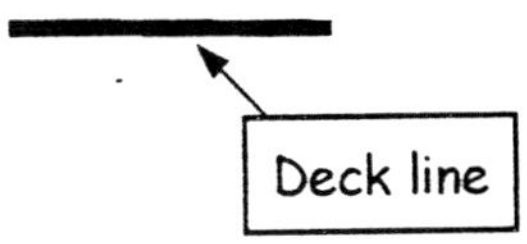

SW...Saltwater
FW...Freshwater
MS...Midsummer
S...Summer
I...Intermediate
W...Winter

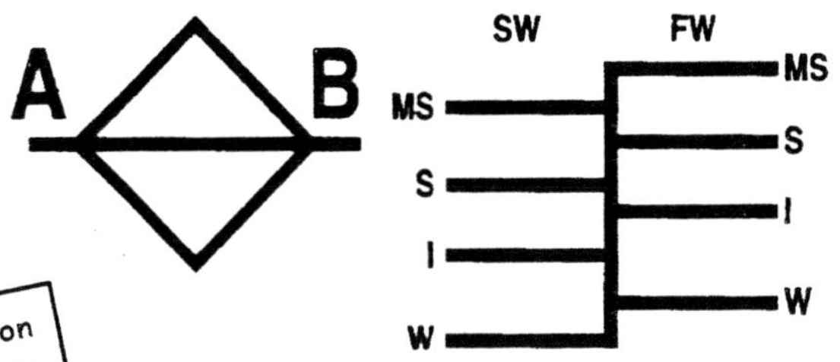

International Load-Lines

A...Deck Line
B...Tropical Freshwater
C...Freshwater
D...Tropical Water
E...Summer Water
F...Winter Water

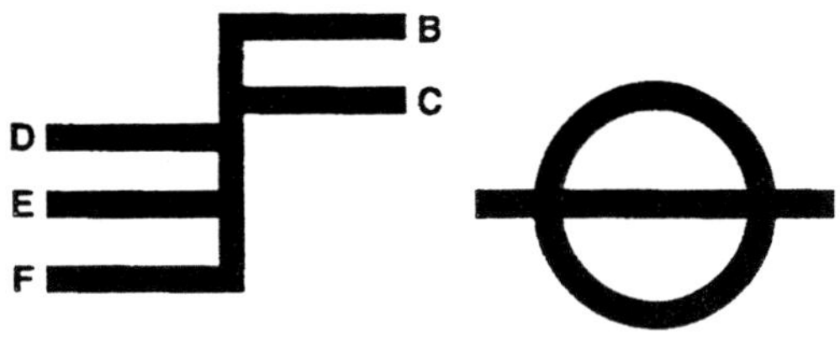

Depending on how the ship is trimmed, there could be differences in draft from the bow to the stern.

Great Lakes Load-Lines

Great Lakes Load-Lines show basically the same information about how the ship is loaded but with more lines for fresh water. The letters on either side of the bisecting line of the diamond indicate the initials for the registering agency or society for the country. In the case above it is The American Bureau of Shipping.

Draft Marks

The draft marks of a ship are painted on the bow (or stem) and stern of the hull. It shows the depth of the keel remaining below the waterline.

Each large number is 6" high. When the waterline is at the base of the large number, there is exactly that number of feet of keel below the waterline. When the water line is at the top edge of a large number, there is exactly that number plus 6" below the waterline.

See the activity, "Float an Egg" page 34, for more fun about the differences in floating in salt and fresh water.

Does your boat have load lines?

Draft Marks

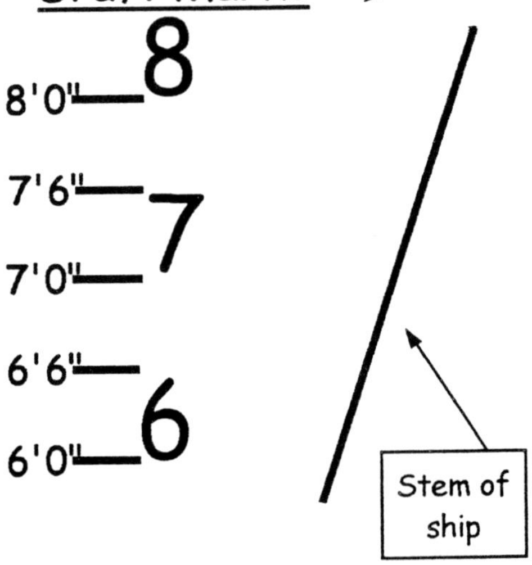

Pirates!

Play the Fun Afloat version of Battleship. Sink your opponent's armada or find his hidden chest of gold to win the game before he does the same to you!

Extra Cargo Needed
Photocopy of playing charts from Compartment A of the Cargo Hold

Getting Underway

Goal

Be the first to sink your opponent's armada or find his gold to win the game. Players take turns attacking their opponent's ships. If one of your cannons hits the spot where your opponent has hidden his stash of gold, you instantly win.

Play

Each player has two 10x10 grid charts. One chart keeps track of where your own ships are and your opponent's hits and misses. The other chart is for marking your own hits or misses and your opponent's ships you sink. You can make your own charts using graph paper or you can photocopy the playing page from Compartment A of the Cargo Hold.

Without your opponent seeing, draw in your 4 ships on your chart by coloring in squares for each ship.

- Square Rigger: 5 squares
- Galleon: 4 squares
- Galleon: 4 squares
- Longboat: 2 squares

Ships can be placed vertically, horizontally, or diagonally. Outline each ship so that they can be identified easier. Next draw in your stash of gold. Place a large G in the square you choose. Place a large book or other barrier to hide your charts from each other or cover your chart and keep it hidden.

Decide who will go first. Then take turns firing cannonballs and trying to sink a ship by calling out a coordinate where you think your opponent has hidden a ship. Call the letter coordinate first, then the number coordinate. See page 92 for an example game. *(continued next page)*

Play (Continued)

Both players keep track of all hits or misses on the 2 charts by using an 0 for misses and an X for hits. By crossing out ship names below the chart as they are sunk, each player can tell what ships are left to sink. If a player calls out the coordinates for his opponent's gold, that player instantly wins. The first person to sink his opponent's ships or captures his opponent's gold wins the game.

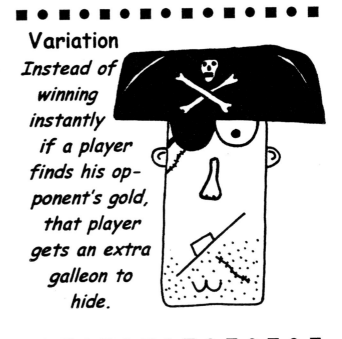

Variation

Instead of winning instantly if a player finds his opponent's gold, that player gets an extra galleon to hide.

Example

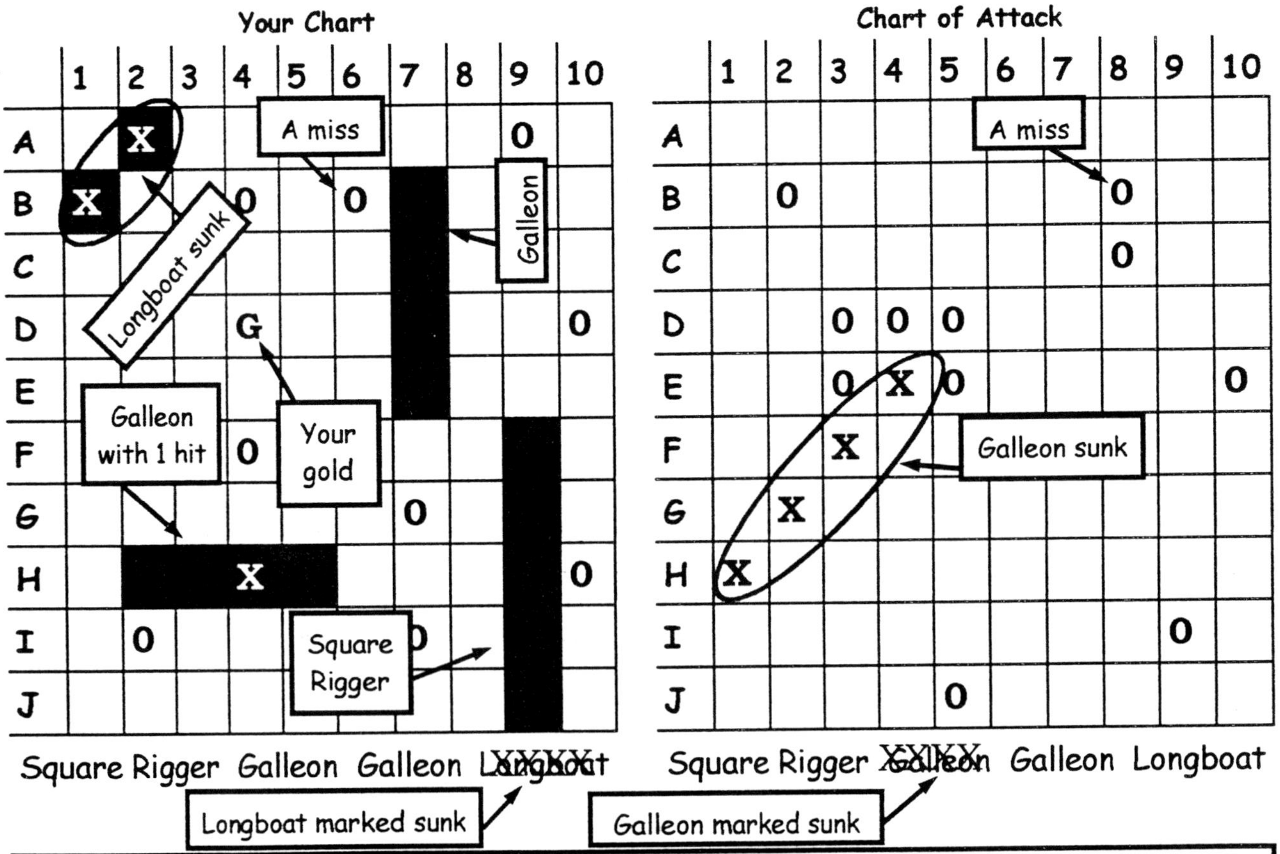

As you can see from this example, you have sunk one of your opponent's galleons and he has sunk your longboat.

Message in a Bottle

Explore the currents in the area you are boating with help from strangers that find your messages in bottles.

Extra Cargo Needed

Bottles with tight fitting caps or corks
Newspaper
Acrylic paint

Getting Underway

The activity of releasing a bottle with a message into the ocean to catch currents and see where it ends up is an old favorite. But, these days not many beach combers seem to respond to messages in bottles any more. So, this activity is designed to try to catch the eye of beachcombers and entice them to see if there is a message in the bottle they find.

Pick bottles that have a pretty or unusual shape. Lay out newspaper before painting. Then decorate them using your acrylic paints in attention getting colors and designs.

To attract attention, use simple flashy designs to decorate your bottle.

You could even paint messages on the outside like, "Open me Please!" or "Message Inside!"

On the bottom of each bottle, paint an identification number so that you will know which bottle was found when you hear back from the finder. In the back of one of your journals, make note of where each one was released. Then, if you get a response from someone, record where it was found and any other information given.

The message you include should entice someone to respond. In your message write where and when you released the bottle so that the finder will learn about currents, too. Include a photocopy of the response form from Compartment A of the Cargo Hold that can be filled out and easily sent back. You can even put in a dollar bill to entice someone to respond.

Don't forget your Identification # on the bottom if you are sending out more than one!

Analyzing the Information

Make a guess as to where your bottle will be found by studying the currents and wind that would influence your bottle's movement.

On your chart or map of your area, mark the spot where you released each bottle. Then, when you receive notice that someone found a bottle, mark where it was found. Use dividers to measure how far your bottle traveled in the time it took from launch to recovery. You could even calculate it's average speed of travel though it could have been washed up on the beach for quite a while.

Include a few words in your message asking the finder to recycle the bottle when done.

You never know who will find your bottle!

Draw it Before you See it

Draw a picture of the approach to a harbor before you even see it with the help of a contour-lined chart.

Extra Cargo Needed
Chart with contour lines
Nautical Chart No. 1

Chart No. 1 will help you learn what the different chart symbols mean.

Getting Underway

On a chart with contour lines marked on the land, pick a harbor you will be visiting soon. Find out from which direction you will be approaching the harbor and think about how it will look as you approach.

Lines on the chart that are drawn very closely together mean that the topography is very steep. As lines get further apart, the land becomes less steep. Places without lines show plateaus or flat areas.

Check for islands that may be in the area and how they will appear. Look at the curvatures of the islands and shoreline in the area. And, search for landmarks like smoke stacks, bridges, spires, or even lighthouses that will need to be in your picture. Hold the chart at an angle in the direction you will be approaching to get an idea of what you will see first as you get close.

Drawing and Comparing

Now try to draw what you will see as you approach the harbor. Remember to include any landmarks, islands, rocky outcrops, etc. Even include the surrounding vegetation if you can find information about it. On the pages that follow, you will find information about some important chart symbols that can help you with your drawing.

Bring your drawing out when you get near the area of the harbor and try to find the different landmarks. How close are you to the real view? Try this activity several times as you get better at chart reading and navigating.

From DMA Chart #21602 Approaches to the Panama Canal

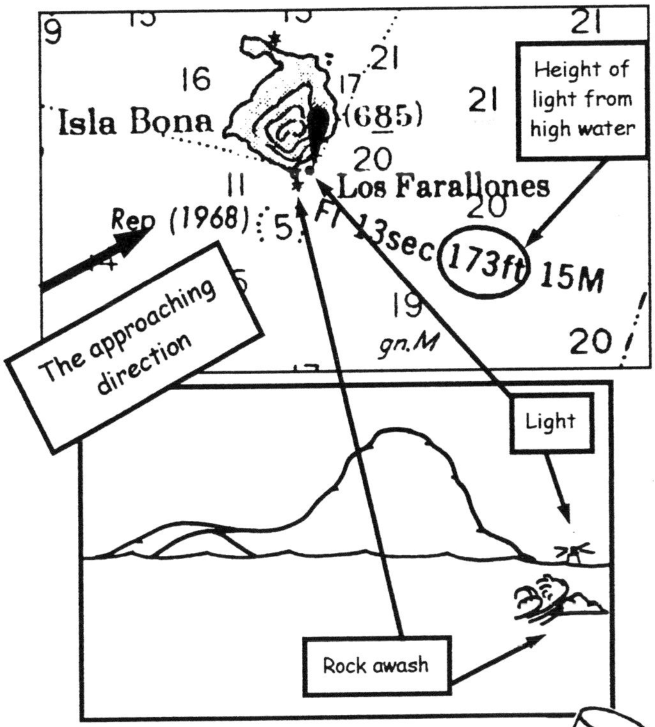

Projected drawing from chart

Some Basic Chart Symbols for Coastlines and Heights from Chart No. 1 U.S.A. Nautical Chart Symbols Abbreviations and Terms

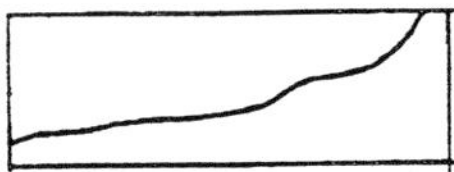	*Coastline, surveyed*	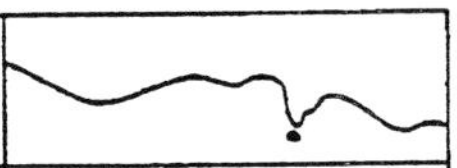
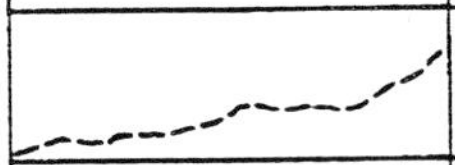	*Coastline, unsurveyed*	
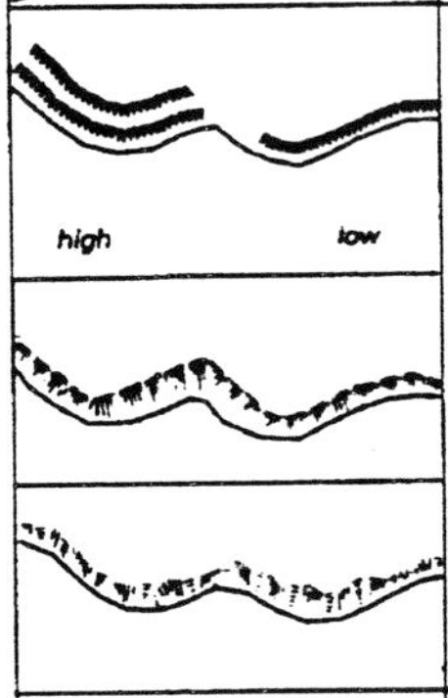	*Steep coast, Steep coast with rock cliffs, Cliffs*	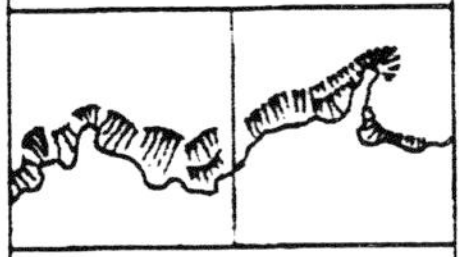
	*Coastal hillocks, elevation not determined*	
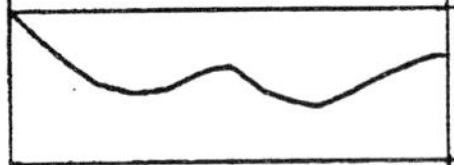	*Flat coast*	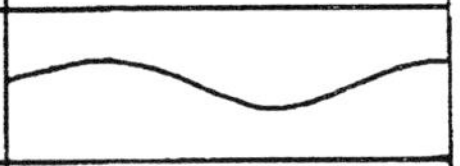
	*Sandy shore*	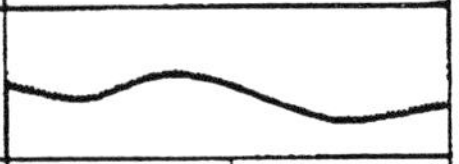
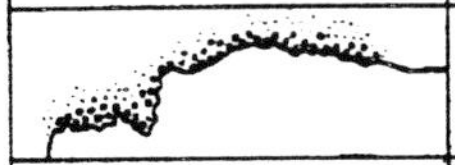	*Stony shore, Shingly shore*	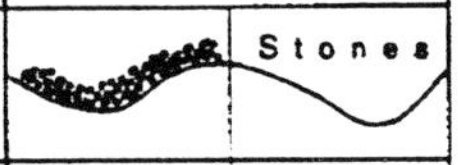
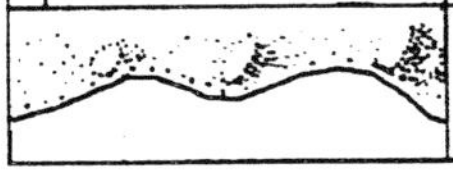	*Sandhills, Dunes*	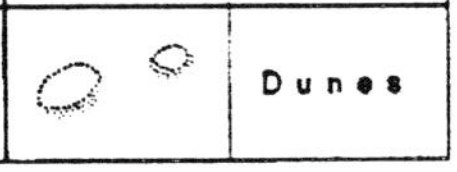

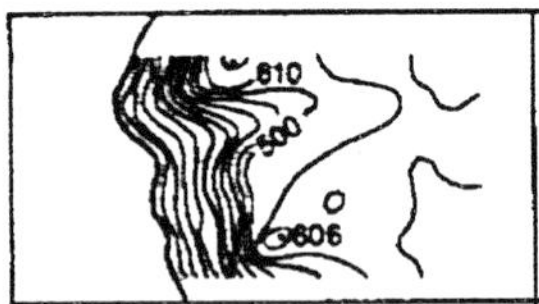	*Contour lines with spot heights*	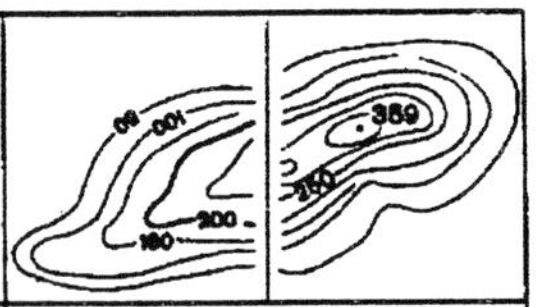
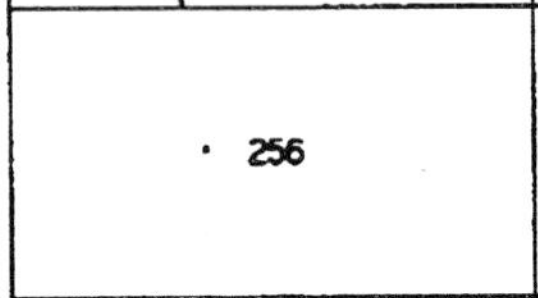	*Spot heights*	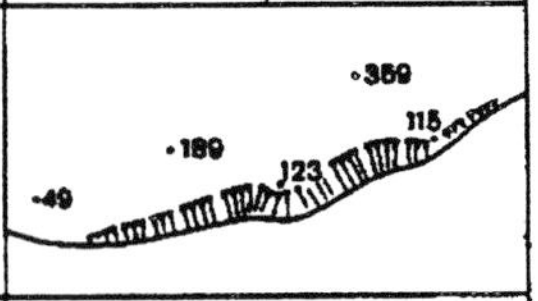
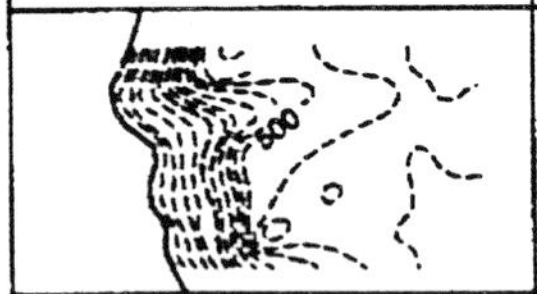	*Approximate contour lines with approximate heights*	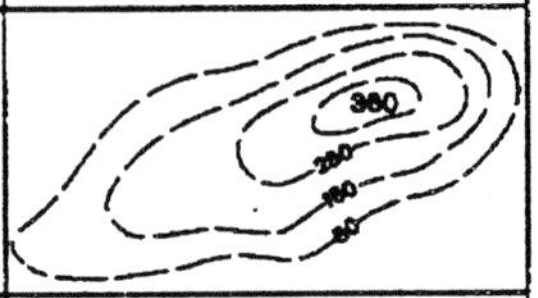
	*Form lines with spot heights*	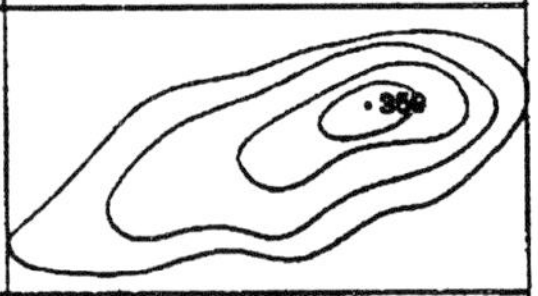
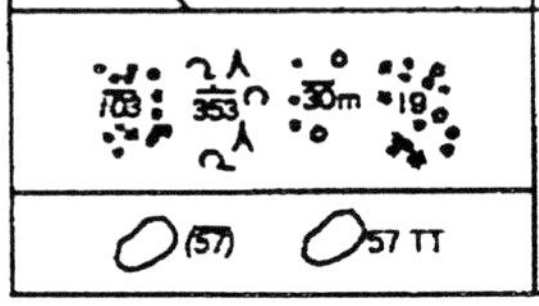	*Approximate height of top of trees (above height datum)*	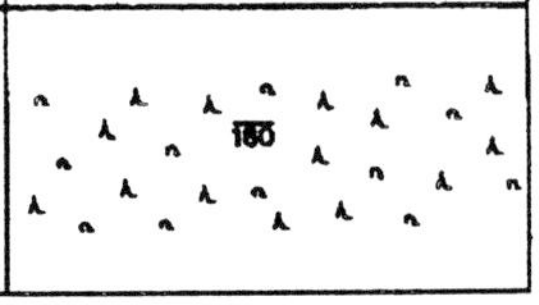

	Rubble
	Hachures
	Shading
	Lagoon
Wooded	*Deciduous woodland*
Wooded	*Coniferous woodland*
	Tree plantation
Cultivated	*Cultivated fields*
Grass	*Grass fields*
Rice	*Paddy (Rice) fields*
Bushes	*Bushes*

Coast Pilots

Coast Pilots published by the National Ocean Service give a wealth of information for the areas they cover. If you have one for the area you are boating, use it to find out about the place you are drawing. Sometimes it will describe vegetation and terrain. It will also have information on obstructions, bridges, towers seen from the water, etc.

	River, Stream	Name
	Intermittent river	
	Rapids, Waterfalls	
	Lakes	

A Practice Chart

For practice or in case you don't have a chart with contour lines, here is an island in Panama you can try to draw. You can imagine approaching it from any angle you would like. But, watch out for those rocks!

The number 610 on the island represents its highest elevation.

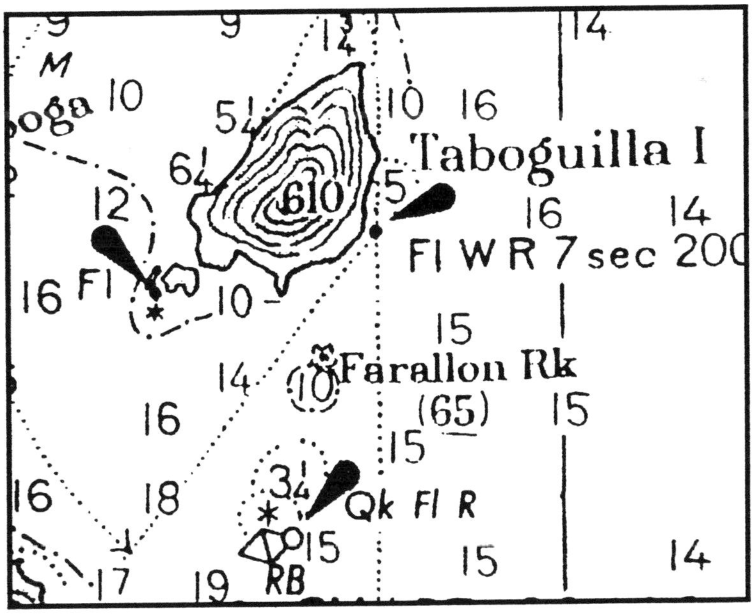

From DMA Chart #21602 Approaches to the Panama Canal

Design a Boat from Trash

Trash aboard your boat can accumulate rapidly. Use your imagination and that trash to design a boat to experiment with while swimming or in a basin.

Ideas

- Nut shells make ideal hulls for model boats. Fasten a toothpick mast with a label sail and test your creation in the wind.
- Experiment with foam trays, tin cans, thread spools, liter pop bottles, etc. as boat hulls.
- Straws can make wonderful masts or can be cut down to make perfect tiny boats to race in a basin regatta.

Don't let your creations get away to become flotsam!

Getting Underway

Let your imagination soar as you look through that trash bag for suitable hulls and other boat parts. Wash out whatever pieces you chose, lay out some newsprint to protect your workplace, and create.

When you have decided on your basic design and have a hull, test it in a basin or bucket and modify it as needed. Small holes or cracks can be sealed with silicone.

Don't be afraid to try new ideas; it is your creation after all. Remember to clean up after yourself!

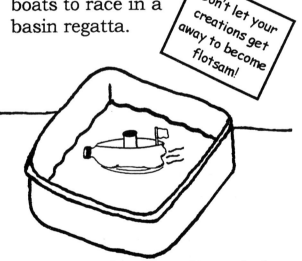

Take your boat out for a sea trial in your basin or bucket!

Don't get too discouraged if some of your boat designs turn over or sink during trials. Some of the best inventions started out as flops.

Make an Underwater Viewer

Waves and floating debris make it hard for anyone to see into the water at any depth. Only the clearest of waters and glassy seas allow an aquarium view of the underwater world. But, with your own underwater viewer, you can have an aquarium view from your dinghy.

Extra Cargo Needed
- Empty coffee can
- Can opener
- Metal file
- Plastic wrap
- 2 rubber bands

Getting Underway

Cut the bottom out of the can with your can opener.

Carefully file all edges smooth, then clean it out well.

Stretch a piece of plastic wrap over the bottom edge and secure it in place with the two rubber bands around the can, one inch apart.

With the open end down, pull the sides of the plastic wrap down to eliminate any creases or sags. Don't pull so tight that the plastic wrap breaks.

Turn it over and there is your underwater viewer!

WATCH OUT! While using your viewer near the water, always wear your life jacket. Stay low. And, keep most of your weight in the boat or on the dock.

Using your Viewer

While close to the water on a dock or in your dinghy, put your viewer into the water being careful not to put it in deeper than the rubber bands. Put your face up to the open end of the can to cut out any of the sun's glare, and watch the underwater world without snorkeling in the water.

Underwater Viewer

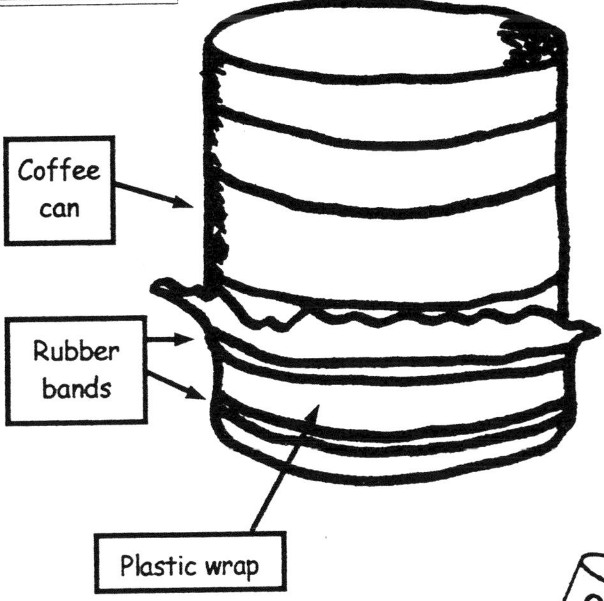

Sunscreen Research

Haven't you ever wondered if your sunscreen is really working? Is one brand better than another? Here's your chance to find out. Design an experiment to test sunscreens while you are out boating.

Extra Cargo Needed

Different brands of sunscreen
Stickers
Sunny day

Remember to have areas on your participants that will not have any sunscreen protection as your control.

Getting Underway

First, enlist the help of crew-members to be your test subjects. Put sunscreen on your test subjects using the arms, legs, and back for testing places. Two different brands or kinds of sunscreen can be tested on two arms while another two are tested on the legs. A washable marker can be used to draw a line down the middle of the back for another two test areas. Put a sticker on an exposed area to compare no sun exposure to the protected and unprotected areas. Limit the exposure of your test participants so that sunburns do not occur. Also, testing should be done during times when solar exposure is not too intense such as during the morning or late afternoon.

Ideas

- Test different brands with the same SPF values.
- Test different SPF values of the same brand sunscreen.
- If your family happens to have different skin types, test the performance of the same brand and SPF value on each skin type.
- Write your participant's name in sunscreen on his/her back.

Marina Journal

Along the same lines as the anchorage journal, keep track of marinas you visit as you travel.

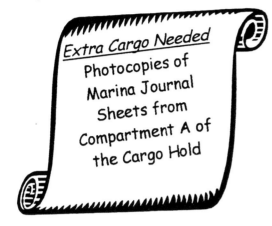

Extra Cargo Needed

Photocopies of Marina Journal Sheets from Compartment A of the Cargo Hold

Getting Underway

Each time you visit a marina, document information about it for later use when traveling in the area or to help other boaters headed that way. If you are also keeping track of anchorages, you could include your marina journal in the same notebook.

Ideas

- Record the name of the marina.
- List its general location, closest city, the dates you visited, and even the GPS waypoint.
- Describe its proximity to shopping, tourist activities, and transportation available.
- Include a contact name and phone number.
- Document the cost for your boat and a price list if available.
- List the facilities the marina offers.
- Describe the type of docks and docking arrangements.
- Include the weather you encountered during your stay and whether the marina was good protection from storms.
- Give an overall rating for the marina on a scale of 1-10.

See page 171 to order a comb bound Marina/ Anchorage Journal

Take a picture of each marina you visit and put it into your journal. It will help you remember each one later.

Distant Objects

A favorite game when traveling is to guess when you will be alongside a distant object you see. It could be a lighthouse, other tall building, an island or mountain; anything in the distance.

Getting Underway

When a definite object is seen in the distance, each person guesses what time it will be when the boat reaches it. Guesses can be based on any information available. You can use your average speed (see page 21), your kamal to figure your distance away from the object (see page 74), or information from your chart about currents, etc. Or everyone playing could make a wild guess. The closest guess without going past the time is the winner.

Alternate Course

- After you pass your distant object, try to guess when it will totally disappear from view. Does it take the same amount of time? Look for obstructions that may make it disappear sooner than you think.
- For closer objects, try to guess to the nearest second when it will be along side one part of your boat. In this case you can pick smaller objects like buoys, or a log in the water.

As you can see in the picture below, you will only be able to see objects between you and the horizon because of the curvature of the earth.

The higher you are the further you will see. The higher an object, the further away you will be able to see it.

The distance you can see = (1.14)(√your height)
Your height means your height above the water.
You can see 2.3 nm if you are 4 feet above the water.

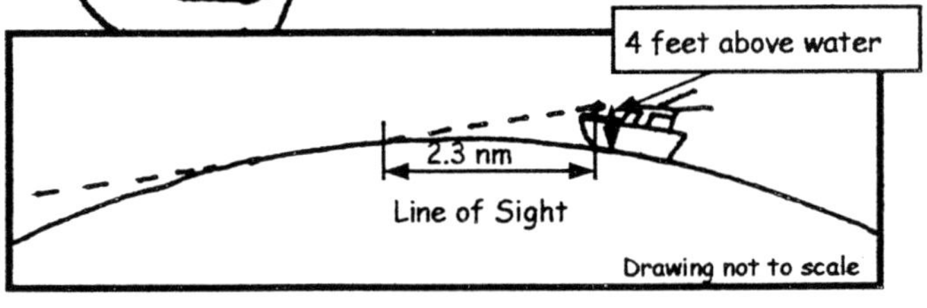

Seaweed Gases

Seaweeds are a major producer of oxygen in our environment. Watch seaweed produce oxygen in a bottle.

Most scientists believe that a majority of our oxygen supply came from ocean plants hundreds of millions of years ago.

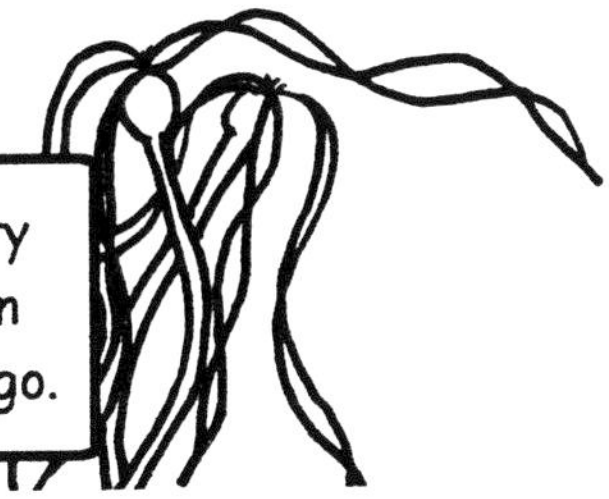

Getting Underway

Gather a clump of living, but floating, seaweed and carefully thread it into your bottle. Add water to about an inch below the top and screw the lid on tightly.

Wedge your bottle sideways in the sun out in the cockpit or somewhere on deck.

Let any sediments or debris settle to the bottom. Then check the seaweed periodically. Look for tiny bubbles coming off of the leaves of the seaweed. This is oxygen that the plant has produced as a by-product of photosynthesis.

Unscrew the lid and breathe in your own small supply of fresh oxygen. But, use caution, it will smell like seaweed.

Seaweeds are simple plants called algae. They produce their own food through a process called photosynthesis where they use sunlight, water, and carbon dioxide to produce sugar. As a result of this process, seaweeds produce oxygen.

When the carbon dioxide is used up in your bottle, the seaweed will no longer make oxygen and will die. Release your seaweed when you are finished watching it.

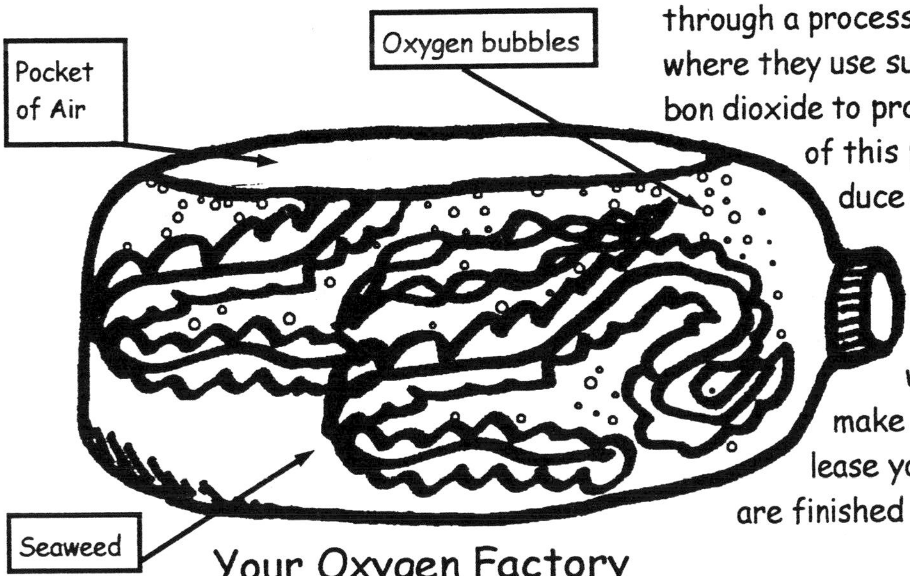

Your Oxygen Factory

Seabird Colony Game

Become the owner of the largest sea bird colony as you travel. This game can be an ongoing game played each time you sail or a shorter game lasting for a one or two day trip.

Getting Underway

As many players as desired can play. While boating, each player announces when they see a sea bird. The first to call out gets that bird as the starting bird for his/her colony. Once everyone has a bird in his/her colony, it is time to watch each colony grow. Use a sheet of paper with each player's name on it to keep track of how the colonies grow.

Certain sightings determine the growth of each person's colony. You will need to decide what sighting will represent one bird being born and what will represent one bird dying. We have used seaweed sightings to represent a birth and a plastic trash bag in the water to represent a death but it depends on the area you are traveling.

If you choose to use buoys, don't use both red and green in the same game. Generally speaking when you see a green buoy, a red buoy will probably be close by to cancel it out.

Ideas

Here are some ideas on what can increase or decrease your colony's population. You can use all, a few, or come up with your own.

One Bird Born	One Bird Dies
Green Buoy	Red Buoy
Cliff	Plastic bag in water
Seaweed	Trash in water
Bridge	Oil spill
Church Spire	Ship
Light House	Smoke stack

As you travel, the first person to call out when an item that represents a baby bird born is sighted adds that baby to his/her colony. The first to call out when an item is sighted that represents a bird dying does **not** subtract a bird from his/her colony, but all the other players do. Play continues for as long as desired.

Boat Journal

The one basic characteristic of boaters is that they love to see and watch other boats. Keeping a boat journal is fun and could be helpful to others trying to find a fellow traveler.

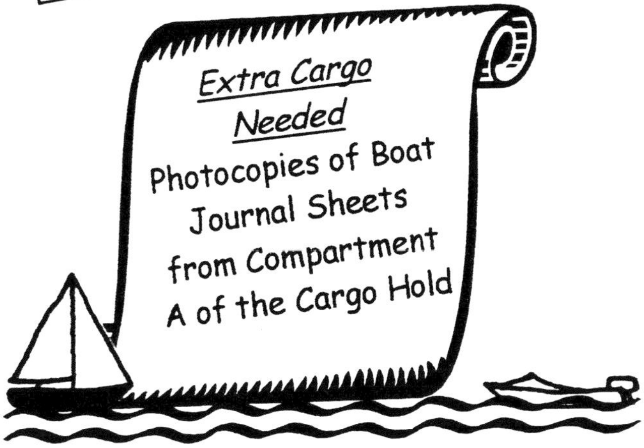
Extra Cargo Needed
Photocopies of Boat Journal Sheets from Compartment A of the Cargo Hold

Ideas

- ☐ Record the names of boats/ships you see.
- ☐ Describe what type of boat or ship it is.
- ☐ List the number of crew aboard.
- ☐ Include their home port and destination. Then document each port where you see them.
- ☐ Reserve a place for boat cards.

Getting Underway

To help you remember names for all those faces you meet aboard boats, track the boats and people you meet as you travel. Not only is it interesting to document, you may end up helping someone by providing information about the last place you saw an overdue boat and crew. The information may also help other boaters keep in touch.

People can be very creative when they name their boats. It's fun to document the boat names you have encountered, too.

If any of the boaters you meet happen to be ham radio operators, include their call sign in your journal.

You can order a comb bound Boat Journal on page 171.

Alternate Courses

- ☸ Survey boaters you meet about the basic equipment they have aboard to find out what the average boater brings along.
- ☸ The number of boats/ships at each harbor in which you stop can be tracked in your Anchorage Journal.
- ☸ Record the nationalities of boats you see in your Flag Journal.

Use Depth to Navigate

Sometimes mariners forget to fully use the information on a chart to navigate. Following a depth curve on your chart with your depth sounder can help you get where you want to go. Practice in a harbor with a dinghy and your sounding lead or with your mother ship.

Getting Underway

When boating in areas that have a consistent slope with no hazards in the way, you can navigate easily by following a depth curve. Study your chart of your local harbor or bay to see if it has a uniform slope. The chart in figure 1 shows curved lines indicating particular depths that can be followed.

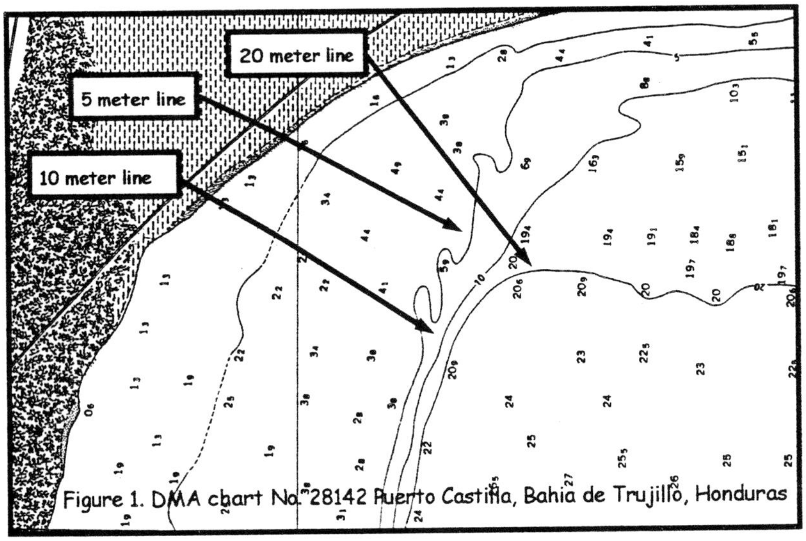

Figure 1. DMA chart No. 28142 Puerto Castilla, Bahia de Trujillo, Honduras

Once you find a contour line that you can follow, take to your boat and try to find that depth. With someone posted at the depth sounder or using your sounding lead, slowly follow that depth curve for as long as safely possible. The person monitoring the depth continuously calls out the depth. The helmsman keeps watch over the chart to know which direction to take to follow the depth curve.

Go slowly so you can change direction when required. Make sure there are no hazards in your way. Remember to watch for fishing buoys, other boats, etc.

Depth sounders use ultrasonic pulses to find the depth of the water. They measure the roundtrip time it takes for the pulses to bounce off the bottom and return to the boat.

Make a Submersible

Create your own little submarine to dive into your tiny bucket of ocean.

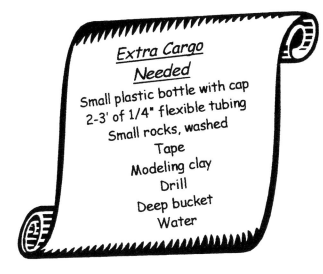

Extra Cargo Needed

Small plastic bottle with cap
2-3' of 1/4" flexible tubing
Small rocks, washed
Tape
Modeling clay
Drill
Deep bucket
Water

Getting Underway

Fill your bucket with water while in your cockpit or on deck. Put your bottle into the water and add only enough rocks to make it begin to sink. Take the bottle out.

Drill two holes into the cap that are slightly smaller than your flexible tubing. You want to make the tubing fit snugly into the holes.

Cut a piece of tubing about twice the height of your plastic bottle. With the rocks inside, cap the bottle and twist the smaller piece of tubing down through one of the holes in the cap. Push the tubing down until it extends to the top of the rocks. Tape the tubing to the side of the bottle. See figure 1.

Twist the remaining longer piece of tubing down into the remaining hole and have it extend inside about an inch.

Push a small ring of clay around each hole to create a airtight seal. Take your submersible to your testing pool (the bucket) and let it float in the water while holding onto the longer piece of tubing.

Slowly suck air out of the submersible through the long tube. This will cause the shorter piece to draw water into your submersible causing it to sink. To bring your submersible to the surface, blow air into the long tube. This replaces the water with air which makes your submersible rise.

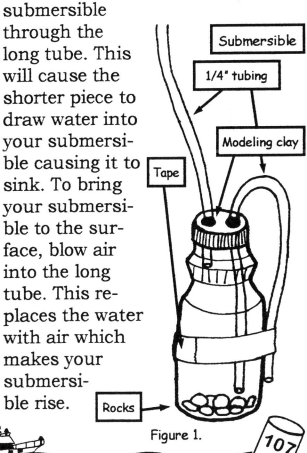

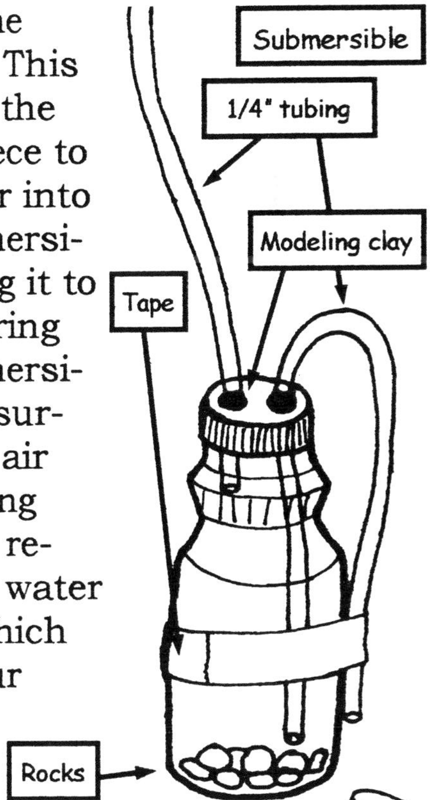

Figure 1.

A type of submersible called a bathyscaphe set a world record descent in 1960. The *Trieste* descended to 35,810 ft. in the Mariana Trench. The pressure the submersible withstood at that depth was 1.17 metric tons/sq. cm.

A Real Submarine

The submersible you made works much like a real submarine. Submarines have ballast tanks that are filled with seawater to reduce their buoyancy and help them sink. When surfacing, compressed air is forced into the ballast tanks forcing the seawater out and causing the submarine to rise to the surface.

The average depth of the Atlantic Ocean is 13,000 feet!

Alternate Courses

- Put a magnet in the bottom of the bottle and try to pick up paper clips or small nails that you have dropped in your bucket of water.
- If you are a swimmer, go swimming with your submersible and watch it rise and sink in the water.

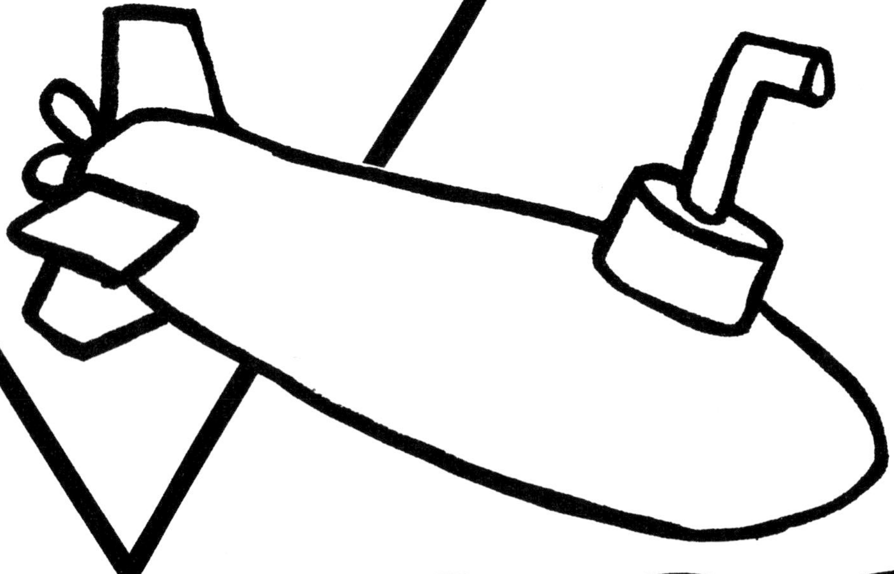

Make a Hydrophone

Record and listen to the sounds beneath the surface with your own underwater microphone!

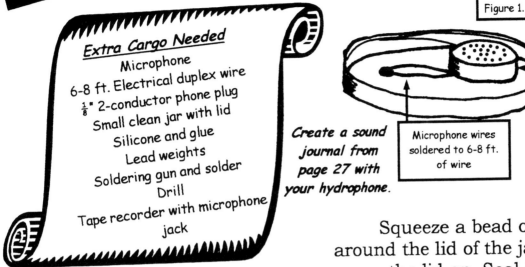

Extra Cargo Needed

Microphone
6-8 ft. Electrical duplex wire
$\frac{1}{8}$" 2-conductor phone plug
Small clean jar with lid
Silicone and glue
Lead weights
Soldering gun and solder
Drill
Tape recorder with microphone jack

Create a sound journal from page 27 with your hydrophone.

Figure 1.

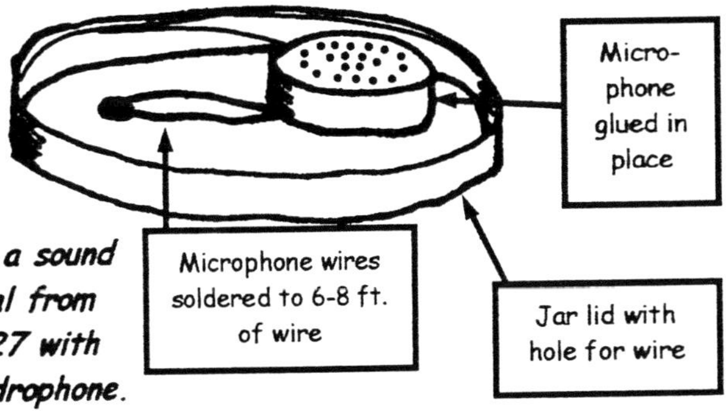

Getting Underway

In a bucket of water, find out how many lead weights are needed to sink your jar with the lid on tight. Take the weights out of your jar and squeeze some silicone into the bottom. Press the weights into the silicone before it cures. Drill a hole the size of your wire near the edge of your jar lid.

Feed your wire through the hole from the outside to the inside of the lid and solder it to the small leads on the microphone. See figure 1.

Glue the microphone to the lid fitting it so that no wires will get in the way of the lid closing onto the jar. Make sure the diaphragm part of the microphone will be facing out into the jar.

Squeeze a bead of silicone around the lid of the jar and screw the lid on. Seal the wire hole with silicone as well. Let the silicone dry thoroughly.

Solder the other end of the wire to the phone plug leads. Plug into the microphone jack of the tape recorder. (Continued)

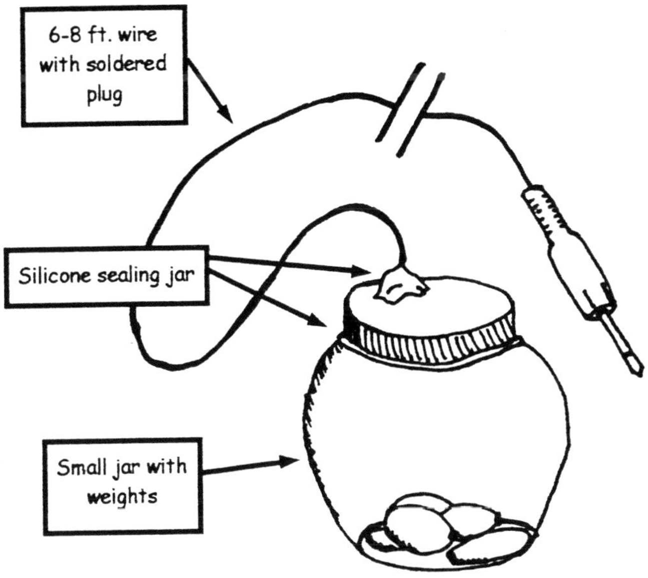

Finished Hydrophone

What you Might Hear

- Dolphins and whales make clicking sounds when echo-locating.
- Snapping shrimp make loud popping sounds when defending their territory.
- As they prepare to lunge at fish, dolphins will sometimes make a sudden bang to scare their prey.
- Propellers from other boats make a whine that changes in pitch when the speed of the propeller varies.
- Whales and dolphins make singsong sounds when communicating to each other.

Using your Hydrophone

After the sealant has cured, you are ready to record. Hang your hydrophone over the side a few feet into the water while it is plugged into the tape recorder. Record the sounds in the water beneath you. Then rewind the tape and listen.

Your hydrophone should not be dragged in the water as you travel but used when the boat is completely stopped, otherwise the wires will get pulled out.

Anytime you see animal life in the water, try out your hydrophone and listen in to the underwater world!

Seaweed for Dinner?

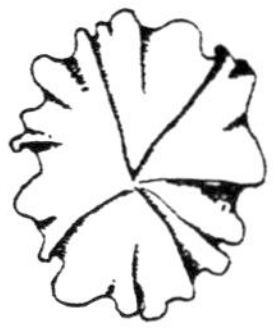

Seaweed is eaten by millions of people yet it still is seen as an oddity by many. Be a member of the Fun Afloat Tastee Club and give seaweed a try!

Getting Underway

Seaweed is a popular food all over the world. Most kinds are high in vitamins and minerals

You can gather your own seaweed to eat. There is a short identification guide in Compartment A of the Cargo Hold to help you. Nori, dulse, or sea lettuce can be washed and dried on a line in the sun. Then they can be broken up and sprinkled into salads or soups. Or, sprinkle dried seaweed on hot rice with soy sauce and lemon pepper.

Gathering Seaweed

Though most seaweeds are edible, be careful only to gather those that are marked edible in an identification guide.

By gathering fresh looking floating seaweed in areas that are abundant, you will be helping to keep the seaweed population healthy. Don't harvest the seaweeds that are still attached unless you are in an area of great abundance.

Don't gather seaweeds near industrial plants or heavily populated areas where the water is not pristine.

Wash all seaweed with clean water before eating. See the next page for some seaweed recipes. Be adventurous! Serve up some seaweed!

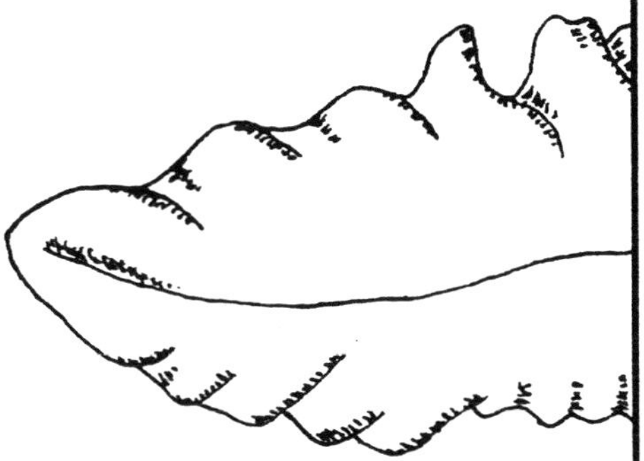

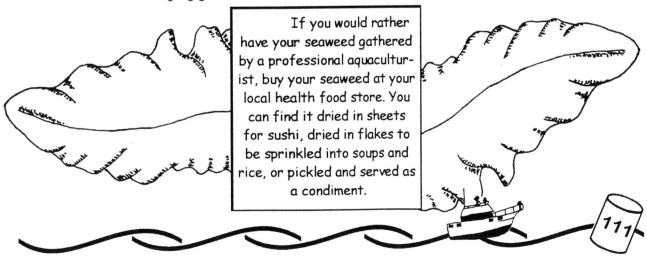

If you would rather have your seaweed gathered by a professional aquaculturist, buy your seaweed at your local health food store. You can find it dried in sheets for sushi, dried in flakes to be sprinkled into soups and rice, or pickled and served as a condiment.

Seaweed Recipes

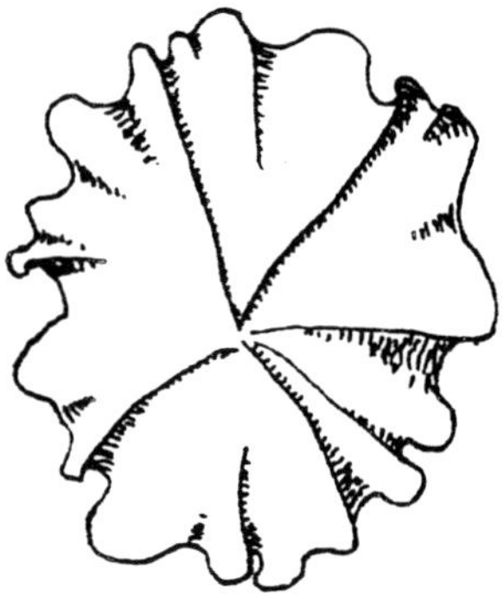

Purple laver or nori

Pan Sautéed Nori

Let your fresh nori dry on a line overnight, then boil in fresh water for a few minutes and drain on paper towels. Chop into bite size pieces and sauté in oil with a sprinkle of lemon pepper. Serve with rice.

Seaweed Pudding

1/4 cup dried Irish moss (carragheen)
2 cups milk (soy milk can be substituted)
Sugar and vanilla to taste

Add dried Irish moss to milk in a double boiler and cook for about 25-30 minutes. Strain, then add sugar and vanilla to taste. Cool and serve.

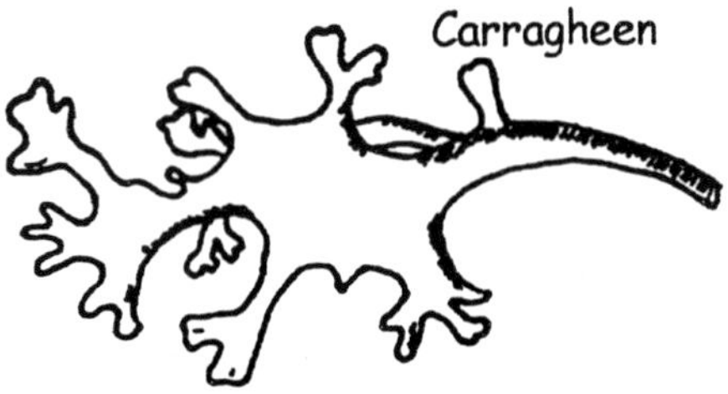

Carragheen

Sushi with Fresh Nori

Fresh nori
Cooked sushi rice
Cucumber strips
Avocado strips
Cooked fish or shrimp

Let your fresh nori dry overnight on a line, then boil for a few minutes in fresh water and rinse in cold water. Lay out your leaf on a sheet of wax paper on the counter. Spread cooked rice over the seaweed. Then on one end, lay strips of avocado, cucumber, and your fish or shrimp.

Carefully roll into a log shape and cut into wheel shapes with a clean moist knife. Serve with wasabi and pickled ginger.

See the Cargo Hold Compartment B for a short identification guide to seaweeds.

Card Games

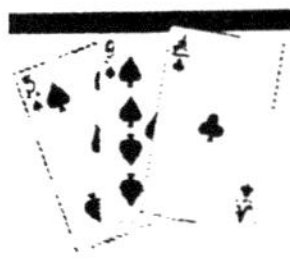

Here are a few favorite card games to play while aboard!

Go Fish!

Players: 2-6 people
Object: Collect the most sets of cards to win.
Deal: Each player is dealt 5 cards. The remaining cards are stacked in the middle as the fishing pond.
Play: Starting with the youngest player and proceeding to the left, each player in turn asks another player by name to give up all of his cards of a specific rank. "Judy, give me all of your threes." The rank requested must be one that the asker has at least one of in his hand. If the player that has been asked has one or more of this rank, he must give up **all** of them. If the requested player does not have any cards of that rank, he answers, "Go fish." This means that the player's whose turn it is must draw the top card from the card pile. A player's turn continues as long as he continues to receive cards he has asked for. If told to "go fish," and that player gets the card he asked for from the pile, his turn continues by asking for another rank from another player.

As soon as any player completes a full set of one rank (four of a kind), he shows those cards and lays the set in front of him. The one who collects the most sets when there are no more cards remaining, wins the game.

I Doubt It

Players: 4-12 players
Object: Get rid of all of your cards to win the game.
Deal: 4-5 players use one shuffled deck , 6 or more players use two decks shuffled together. Cards are dealt to everyone until there are no more.
Play: Youngest player begins by placing any number of cards from one to four (one to eight if playing with two decks) face down in the center of the table saying how many cards there are and of what rank. Each player at his turn does the same, explaining the number and rank of the cards he discards into the pile of cards in the center.

The order of the discard starts with aces for the first player, kings for the second player, queens for the third, and so forth down to twos. It then begins again at aces and descends again until someone discards all of his cards.

Each player must disclose the exact number of cards he puts down but the cards need **NOT** be the rank that he announces. The object is to get rid of your entire hand. So, it may be necessary to add cards to the discard not of the rank called for on your turn. But, BE CAREFUL; after each play, any other player may say, "I doubt it!" The person who discarded must show the cards he laid down to prove that he named them correctly. If it is found that he lied, the discarder has to take the whole pile. The doubter takes the whole pile if the announcement and cards match. If two players doubt the discard at the same time, the doubter nearest to the player's left takes precedence.

T-R-A-S-H

 # Players: 4, 6, or 8 in teams of two.
Object: Be the first team to earn enough letters to spell "TRASH."
Deal: Each player is dealt 5 cards. The remaining cards are held to the side by the dealer for use later.
Basics: The object of each hand is to be the first person to get four of a kind (4 aces, or 4 kings, or 4 twos, etc.), signal to your partner, and have your partner yell out "TRASH" and announce that you have four of a kind. You then show your cards to prove your four of a kind and earn a letter to ultimately spell "T-R-A-S-H." Any player can exclaim "TRASH" for any other player if he thinks someone from another team is trying to signal their teammate. If the announcer picks correctly and that player does have four of a kind, then the announcer earns a letter for his team. If the announcer is wrong and the person he picked does not have four of a kind, then a letter is awarded to the other team. If the caller is wrong about his own teammate having four of a kind, a letter is given to all other teams.
Secret Signals: Each team secretly decides on a signal to use whenever one of the team gets four of a kind. All signals have to be visible or audible by all players. Players closely watch their partner and the other players to see a signal so that they can call "TRASH" first.

Play: Play begins when each person discards one card face up into the center of the table . Those cards are available to be picked up by any player and traded for one in hand. For every card picked up, one must be discarded so that there are always four in each person's hand during play.

When no one wants any cards in the center pile, the dealer gathers them up and forms a throw away stack to be shuffled and used later when the deck has been exhausted. The dealer then uses the set aside deck to deal one more card to each player. Each player then discards one card face up into the center and trading commences again. The first person to touch a card gets it to trade with one in his hand. Play continues like this until someone announces "TRASH" and names the person who allegedly has four of a kind. It is then proven whether that person has four of a kind. If the chosen person does not, then play continues as before until a "TRASH" is called successfully. After a successful "TRASH" has been called, all cards are gathered to be shuffled again and dealt out, five to each player. Hands are played until a team manages to earn enough letters to spell "T-R-A-S-H."

Games on the Front and Back Cover

Just in case you don't know how to play the games on the back and front covers of this book, here are the rules for each.

Using the Erasable Boards

📖 Dry erase markers or washable markers work well on the boards (though washable markers smudge more).

📖 Rub with a damp cloth for fresh clean-ups. Spray cleaner applied to the cloth will clean up more stubborn marks.

📖 Damp cotton swabs work well to clean up small areas when mistakes occur during a game.

📖 Blank areas on the boards can be used for score-keeping.

Five in a Row

Number of Players: 2

Object: Be the first to get five marks in a row diagonally, horizontally, or vertically.

Play: Decide who will go first. Using X's and O's or colored-in squares with two different colors, players take turns writing their mark in a square on the grid. Each player tries to block his opponent by putting his mark in a square where his opponent needs to mark to get five in a row. The game ends when one of the players wins by getting five of his marks in a row.

Variation: Try to get six marks in a row or seven marks in a row.

Tic Tac Toe

Number of Players: 2

Object: Get three marks in a row horizontally, vertically, or diagonally.

Play: Decide who will go first. One player uses O's as a mark, and the other player uses X's as a mark. The players take turns making their marks in the squares on the board trying to get three marks in a row diagonally, horizontally, or vertically. The game ends when a player gets three marks in a row or the board is filled making a tie.

Variation: Try to force your opponent to mark three squares in a row.

Squares

Number of Players: 2

Object: Occupy the most squares.

Play: Decide who will go first. Players take turns connecting two dots with a line during their turn, trying to be the one to close in a square. Each time a player closes in a square, he puts his initial inside it to show ownership and gets to connect another two dots until no more squares can be made. When all squares are closed in, each player counts his squares. The player with the most squares wins.

XOXOXOXO

Cross-words

Number of Players: 2

Object: Be the last to add a word to the board. Or, work together and see how full of words you can make the board.

Play: Decide who will go first. The first player writes a word anywhere on the board either horizontally or vertically. The second player can chose to use that word to write another word, or can write in a word on another area of the board.

Rules:

- Whenever words meet up with each other, they must form words as well.
- Words can only be written from left to right or from up to down.

Variation: Play for a score. Each time a player uses another word on the board to form his word, he gets a point. The last person to write a word onto the board gets a bonus of 5 points. Winner is the one with the highest score. Game ends when one player fails to add a word to the board.

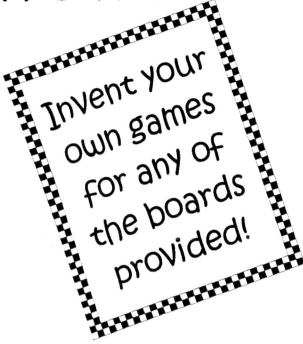

Invent your own games for any of the boards provided!

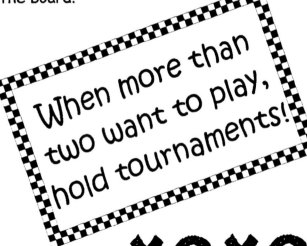

When more than two want to play, hold tournaments!

Doodle Bug

Number of Players: 2

Object: Make funny drawings from a squiggly line.

Play: Decide who will go first. The first player draws a squiggly line. The other player uses that line to complete a drawing, the sillier the better. The second player can draw weird bugs, strange creatures, bizarre landscapes, etc. Players can turn the board around to look at the squiggly line with a new perspective. When one drawing is finished, the second player draws a squiggly line. The game continues as long as the players wish.

XOXOXOXO

The Cargo Hold

Compartment A: Forms and Tables

Flag Journal

Drawing of Flag

Country:

Information learned about country:

Ships/Boats flying Flag:

Flag Journal

Drawing of Flag

Country:

Ships flying Flag: Date:

Passage Log

Date	Hour	Helms-man	Avg. Speed	Avg. Comp. Heading	Distance Since Last	% Cloud Cover	Sea State	Wind Direc.	Wind Speed	Bar. Pres.	Engine Hours	Comments

Passage Log

Date: **Day:** **To:** **From:**

Time	Helmsman	Avg. Comp. Heading	Avg. Speed	Distance Since Last	% Cloud Cover	Sea State	Wind Direc.	Wind Speed	Bar. Press.

Comments:

Distance Log

Date	Time	Weather Conditions	Distance Traveled	Comments

Daily Journal

Date:

Date:

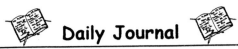

Animal Tracking Table

Date	Time	Position	Species	Total#	Behavior

Animal Tracking Data Sheet	Drawing
Date:	
Species:	
Sea State/Water Color:	
Water Depth:	
Water Temp./Visibility:	
Water Density:	
Wave Height:	
Visibility:	
Air Temperature:	
Wind Velocity/Direction:	
Cloud Cover:	
Position:	
Behavior:	
Grouping:	
Total Number:	
Person Sighting:	

Animal Tracking Sheet
Date and Time:
Species:
Position:
Sea State:
Weather:
Number:
Behavior:
Drawing

Record of Trash Sightings

Date/Time	Position	Composition	Notes

Bottom Topography

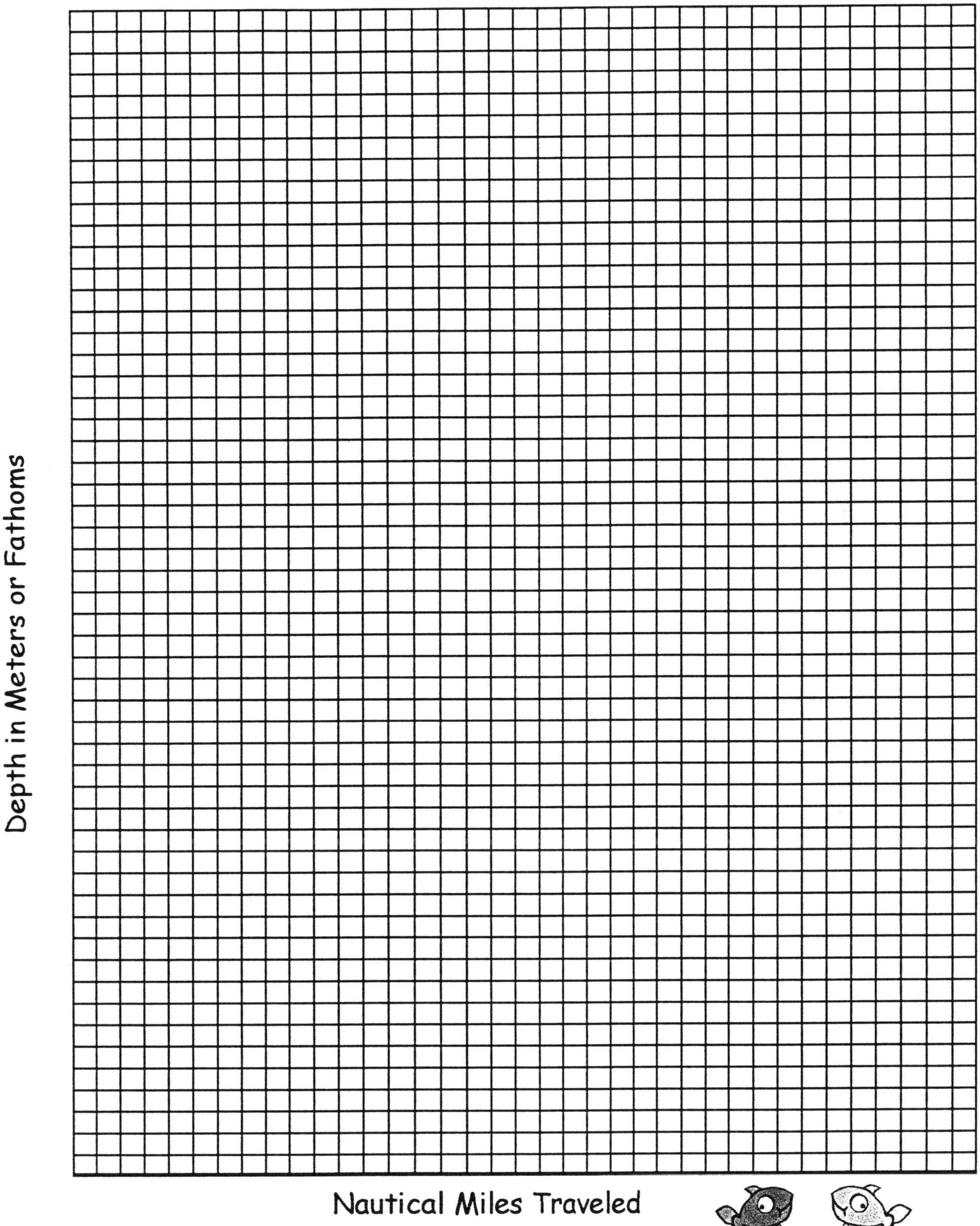

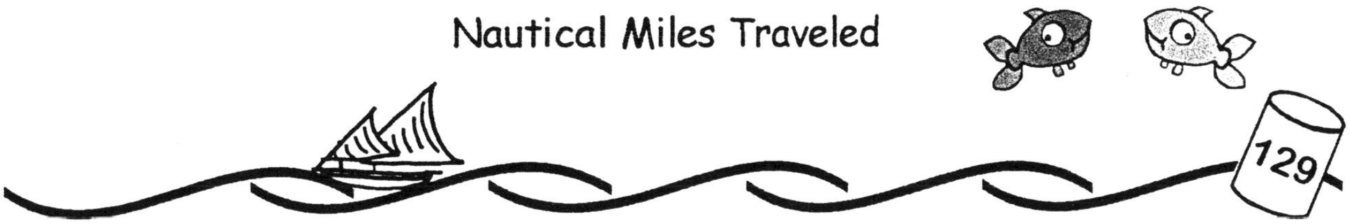

Weather Log

Date/Time	Temp.	Sky	Wind	B.P.	Sea State	Rainfall

Month:

WEATHER LOG

Date	Time	Temp.	Barometric Pressure	Wind Speed	Wind Direction	Cloud Type	%Cloud Cover	Wave Height	Visibility	24 hr. Rain

Long-Trip Hunt List and Score Sheet

Hunt Item	Tally/Score
Dolphins at the bow	
Lightning	
Whale	
Jellyfish	
Flying fish on deck	
Squid on deck	
Another recreational boat	
Rainbow	
Cargo Ship	
Military ship	
Sea turtle	
Sea snake	
Dolphins in the distance	
Retrieved trash	
A day without a course change	
A day without a sail change	

Harbor Hunt List and Score Sheet

Hunt Item	Tally/Score
A plastic bag retrieved	
A fish caught	
Floating seaweed	
Nun buoy	
Can buoy	
Dolphin sighted	
Cargo ship	
Fishing vessel	
Another family boating	
Draw bridge	
Tugboat	
Seagull floating on the water	
Fish jump	
Rain storm in the distance	
Floating log	
Smoke stack	

The Hunt List and Score Sheet

Hunt Item	Tally/Score

Anchorage Journal

Anchorage: **Date:**

Position:

Comments:

Drawing:

Anchorage Journal

Anchorage:	Date:
Position:	
Bottom:	Depth:
Weather:	
Comments:	
Anchorage:	Date:
Position:	
Bottom:	Depth:
Weather:	
Comments:	

Fishing Log

Date	Time	Position	Fish Caught	Length	Weight	Bait/Lure	Line size/Rig	Air Temp.	Moon Phase	Sea State

Fishing Log

Date:	Time:	Position:
Fish Caught:		Size/Weight:
Bait/Lure:		Line/Rig:
Water Temp.:	Visibility:	Density:
Air Temp.:	Visibility:	% Cloud Cover:
Sea State:	Wind Velocity:	Wind Direction:
Date:	Time:	Position:
Fish Caught:		Size/Weight:
Bait Used:		Line/Rig:
Water Temp.:	Visibility:	Density:
Air Temp.:	Visibility:	% Cloud Cover:
Sea State:	Wind Velocity:	Wind Direction:
Date:	Time:	Position:
Fish Caught:		Size/Weight:
Bait/Lure:		Line/Rig:
Water Temp.:	Visibility:	Density:
Air Temp.:	Visibility:	% Cloud Cover:
Sea State:	Wind Velocity:	Wind Direction:
Date:	Time:	Position:
Fish Caught:		Size/Weight:
Bait/Lure:		Line/Rig:
Water Temp.:	Visibility:	Density:
Air Temp.:	Visibility:	% Cloud Cover:
Sea State:	Wind Velocity:	Wind Direction:

Pirates!

	1	2	3	4	5	6	7	8	9	10
A										
B										
C										
D										
E										
F										
G										
H										
I										
J										

Your Chart

Square Rigger Galleon Galleon Longboat

	1	2	3	4	5	6	7	8	9	10
A										
B										
C										
D										
E										
F										
G										
H										
I										
J										

Chart of Attack

Square Rigger Galleon Galleon Longboat

Your Chart

	1	2	3	4	5	6	7	8	9	10
A										
B										
C										
D										
E										
F										
G										
H										
I										
J										

Square Rigger Galleon Galleon Longboat

Chart of Attack

	1	2	3	4	5	6	7	8	9	10
A										
B										
C										
D										
E										
F										
G										
H										
I										
J										

Square Rigger Galleon Galleon Longboat

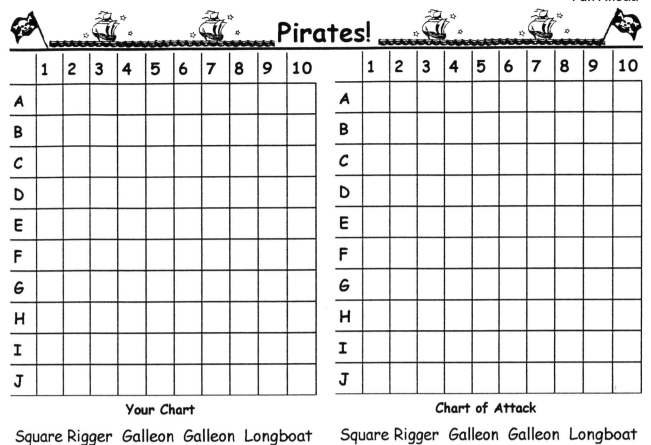

Marina Journal

Marina:	Date:
Location:	
Approach Information:	
Distance to Shopping:	
Distance to Restaurants:	
Contact name:	Phone #:
Price:	
Dock type:	Number:
Weather protection:	
Overall Grade:	
Comments:	

Marina:	Date:
Location:	
Approach Information:	
Distance to Shopping:	
Distance to Restaurants:	
Contact name:	Phone #:
Price:	
Dock type:	Number:
Weather protection:	
Overall Grade:	
Comments:	

Marina Journal

Marina: Date:

Location:

Approach Information:

Comments:

Marina: Date:

Location:

Approach Information:

Comments:

Marina: Date:

Location:

Approach Information:

Comments:

Boat Journal

Boat Name:		Boat Type:
Crew Names:		
Address:		
City:	State/Province:	Postal Code:
E-mail:		
Home Port:		Destination:
Comments:		

Boat Name:		Boat Type:
Crew Names:		
Address:		
City:	State/Province:	Postal Code:
E-mail:		
Home Port:		Destination:
Comments:		

Boat Journal

Boat Name:	Boat Type:
Crew Names:	
Home Port:	
Comments:	
Boat Name:	Boat Type:
Crew Names:	
Home Port:	
Comments:	
Boat Name:	Date:
Crew Names:	
Home Port:	
Comments:	

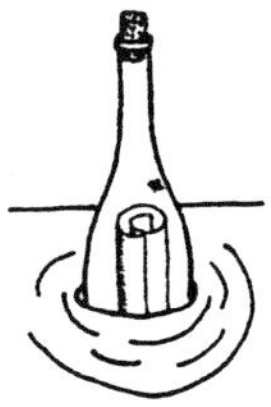

The bottle you found is part of an experiment in currents and communication. Please fill out the response form below and send to the address given. We GREATLY appreciate your reply as well as your beachcombing abilities! THANK-YOU!

Date:		**Date Found:**
Where was this bottle found?		
Identification #:		
What shape was the bottle in?		
Please send this reply to:		
Name:		
Address:		
City:	**State/ Province:**	**Postal Code:**
Country:		
Thank-you for your response! **Please recycle this bottle.**		☺

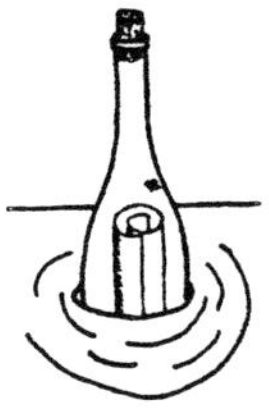

The bottle you found is part of an experiment in currents and communication. Please fill out the response form below and send to the address given. We GREATLY appreciate your reply as well as your beachcombing abilities! THANK-YOU!

Date:		**Date Found:**
Where was this bottle found?		
Identification #:		
What shape was the bottle in?		
Please send this reply to:		
Name:		
Address:		
City:	**State/ Province:**	**Postal Code:**
Country:		
Thank-you for your response! **Please recycle this bottle.**		☺

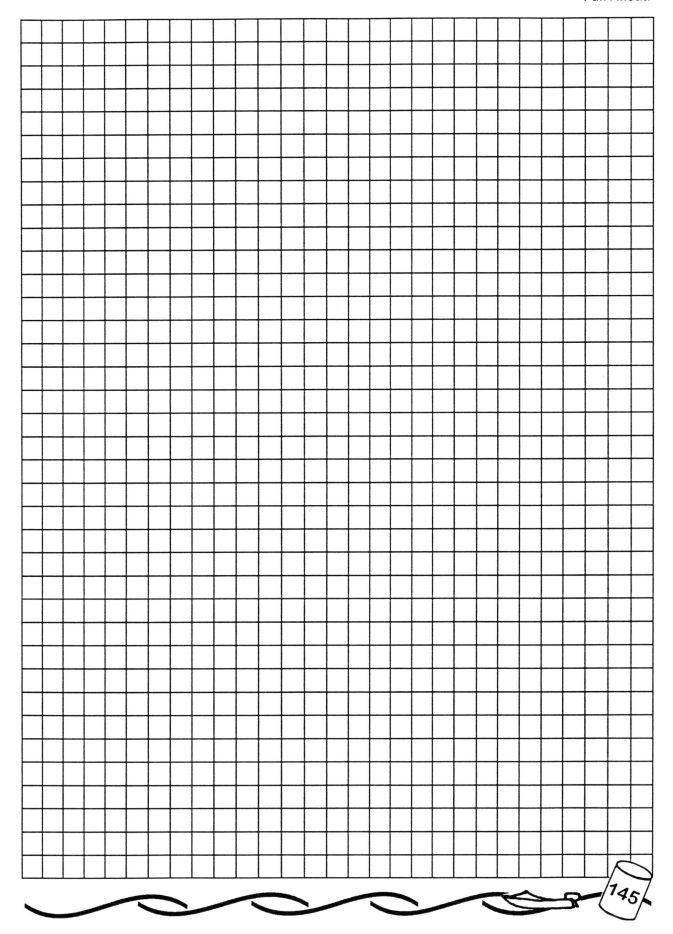

The Cargo Hold

Compartment B: Extra Information and Identification Guides

Approaching Whales

Guidelines

As boaters we have a responsibility to keep ourselves and others safe while we are on the water. This responsibility should extend to include whales and any other marine animals that come within viewing distance of our boats. The United States Marine Mammal Protection Act of 1972 prohibits the harassment, feeding, touching, capture, or killing of any marine mammals with a penalty of up to $25,000 or imprisonment.

Sound Intrusion

You may not realize it but sound travels faster and farther in the water than in air. Cetaceans use sound for communication, foraging for food, and navigation. They have a very good sense of hearing. The potential for disturbing whales with the noise of a vessel approaching is very real. As you approach a whale, slow your engine down. Approach slowly and quietly. Try not to make harsh noises.

Approach Guidelines

Most countries now have whale-watching guidelines to help keep both boaters as well as marine mammals safe. Cetaceans may feel threatened by boats that approach too closely.

Except in the case of Northern Right whales, remain at least 100 yards (the length of a football field) away from cetaceans or other marine mammals. By federal law, each Northern Right whale cannot be approached closer than 500 yards.

Your vessel may not be the only one that encounters the whale(s) you view. Please be aware that the impact of many viewers is cumulative to whales and other marine mammals. Also, whales are more likely to be disturbed when there is more than one boat in the area. If other boats are in the area when you view a whale, communicate with them via radio to establish a plan to take turns approaching.

☞ Never separate a group of whales.
☞ When you need to move your vessel, do so from behind the whale.
☞ Limit your observations to less than $\frac{1}{2}$ hour.
☞ Whales should never be trapped between boats or boats and the shore.
☞ Never pursue a whale.
☞ Avoid being directly in front of a whale.
☞ When a whale shows signs of being disturbed, leave the area. Give them the peace and quiet you would want if you were feeling harassed.

Signs of a Whale being Disturbed

☹ Increased breathing rate
☹ Rapid changes in direction of movement
☹ Loud blowing underwater
☹ Threatening rushes at boat
☹ Tail slapping or tail swishing from side to side

Whale Identification Guide

As a supplement to the many whale identification guides available, we have included an identification guide that shows each whale's dive sequence and blowhole or breath pattern.

Dive Sequences and Breath Patterns

In each series of pictures, the whale is shown preparing to dive. Look at each sequence from right to left. The whale will surface and exhale first, then take in air as it swims close to the surface. The last picture to the left of the sequence shows what you will see last as it dives.

The breath pattern for the baleen whales will have two clouds because they have two blowholes. If a whale is seen from the front, make note that there will be a difference in how the blow looks from the side view shown here. The breath pattern of the only toothed whale shown here, the sperm whale, will have a single cloud since toothed whales have only one blow hole. Wind and sea state can change the effectiveness of identifying a whale this way.

Whales Included

Most of the baleen whales have been included. The Sei and Pygmy Right whales, less documented than the others, are excluded.

The Sperm whale, though it is a toothed whale, is included because of its distinctive blow pattern that is very nearly always to one side.

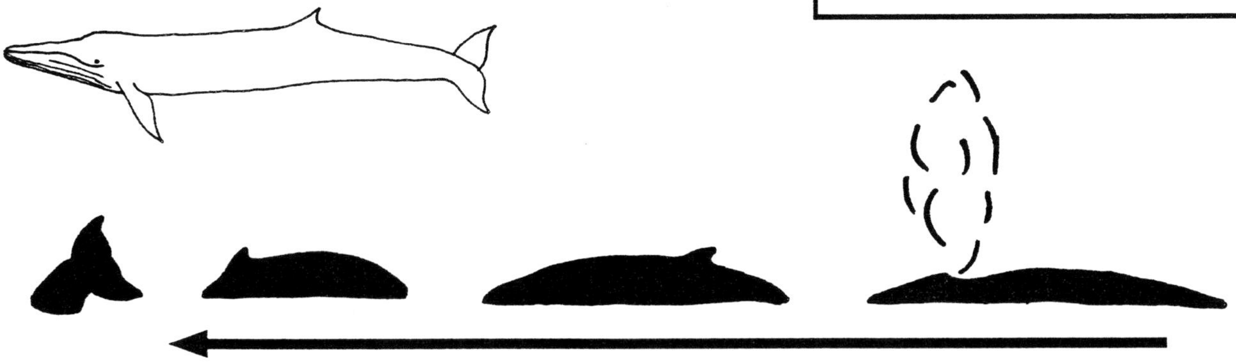

Blue Whale

(Balaenoptera musculus)

Range: In Atlantic from Arctic Circle south to Panama. In Pacific from Chukchi Sea south to Panama.

Size: Up to 110 feet

Probably the largest animal ever known, blue whales are bluish-gray often mottled with gray.

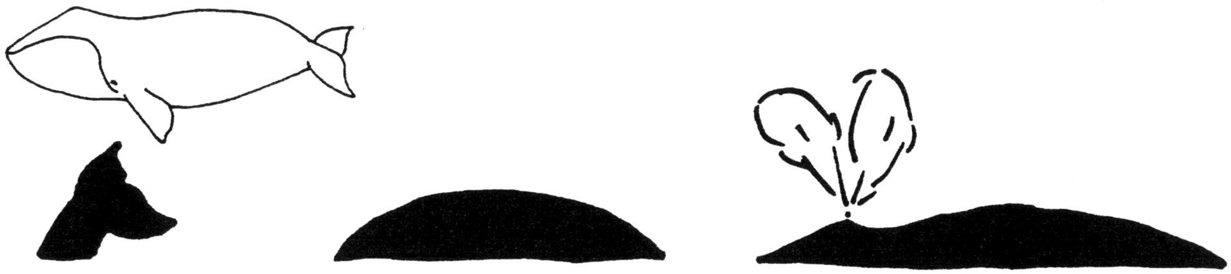

Bowhead Whale
(*Balaena mysticetus*)
Range: In Atlantic off East Greenland. In Pacific throughout the Bering, Chukchi, and Beaufort Seas.
Size: Up to 65 feet
Bowhead whales have a highly arched jaw that allows them to grow the longest baleen of all whales. Individual strips grow to 14 feet! They are the stockiest of the baleen whales with a massive head and white chin patch. Their bodies are bluish-black to bluish gray. They have small paddle-shaped fins and pointed flukes.

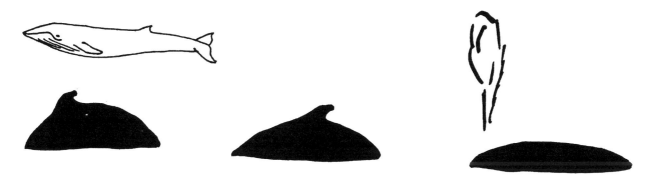

Bryde's Whale
(*Balaenoptera edeni*)
Range: In Atlantic from Virginia to the Caribbean Sea, in Pacific from California to Panama.
Size: up to 46 feet
Also known as Tropical whales, they are normally found close to shore. They seem to travel in loose groups of 5 or 6. As you can see in the dive sequence above, the Bryde's whale does not show its tail fluke when diving. They are dark gray with white on their throats and chins. They also have three ridges on their heads.

Fin Whale
(*Balaenoptera physalus*)
Range: All oceans
Size: up to 78 feet
Fin whales are the second largest of the whales. They are the fastest of the large whales, obtaining bursts of speed of up to 23 mph. They have asymmetrical coloring on the lower jaw; white and creamy yellow on the right side and mottled black on the left. This coloration is believed to be beneficial during their feeding since they have been seen to habitually roll onto their right side to scoop up their catch.

Gray Whale
(*Esrichtius robustus*)
Range: In the Pacific from the Bering and Chukchi seas south to Baja California.
Size: up to 46 feet
Gray whales travel to Baja California every year to calve and breed. Their bodies are mottled with gray and white patches. The head is bumpy with bristly facial hairs. Some have been known to approach whale watching boats and get quite close.

Humpback Whale
(*Megaptera novaeangliae*)
Range: In Atlantic from Northern Iceland south to the West Indies. In Pacific from the Bering Sea south to Southern Mexico.
Size: Up to 53 feet
Humpback whales are mostly black or gray with white on their throats, flippers, and belly. They have the longest flippers of any whale which can be as long as 15 feet. A humpback sometimes feeds by concentrating its food with a bubble curtain that is formed as the whale dives and circles its prey.

Minke Whale
(*Bulaenoptera acutorostrata*)
Range: All oceans
Size: Up to 33 feet
Minke whales are black or dark gray on the back with white bands on the flippers and a white belly. They have a pointed head and a single prominent ridge from their blowholes to the tip of their upper jaw. Make note that the Minke is another whale that does not show its tail fluke during diving.

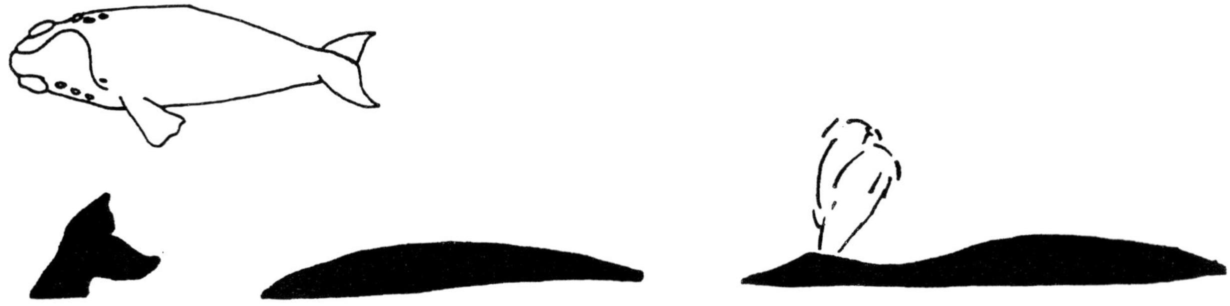

Southern and Northern Right Whale
(*Eubalaena australis* and *Eubalaena glacialis*)
Range: In the Atlantic from Iceland south to Florida. In the Pacific from the Gulf of Alaska south to Central Baja California.
Size: Up to 53 feet.
Right whales are slow swimming black whales that may have patches of white on the belly and chin. They are easy to identify because of their white lumpy patches on their head and jaw that sometimes have barnacles attached.

Sperm Whale
(*Physeter macrocephalus*)
Range: All oceans except the high Arctic.
Size: Up to 65 feet
The blow pattern seen from front or back is distinctively to one side of the of the sperm whale. They are dark gray to black whales with large rectangular heads. Largest of the toothed whales, they feed on giant squid.

Seaweed Identification

Here are some common seaweeds found mainly in the U.S., Canada, and Europe.

In the descriptions of the seaweeds, it has been noted when a seaweed is edible.

(*Rhodophyllis dichotoma*)
Rosy-red to purple-red easily identified with small flat blades 2-5 inches long lined with tooth-like projections.

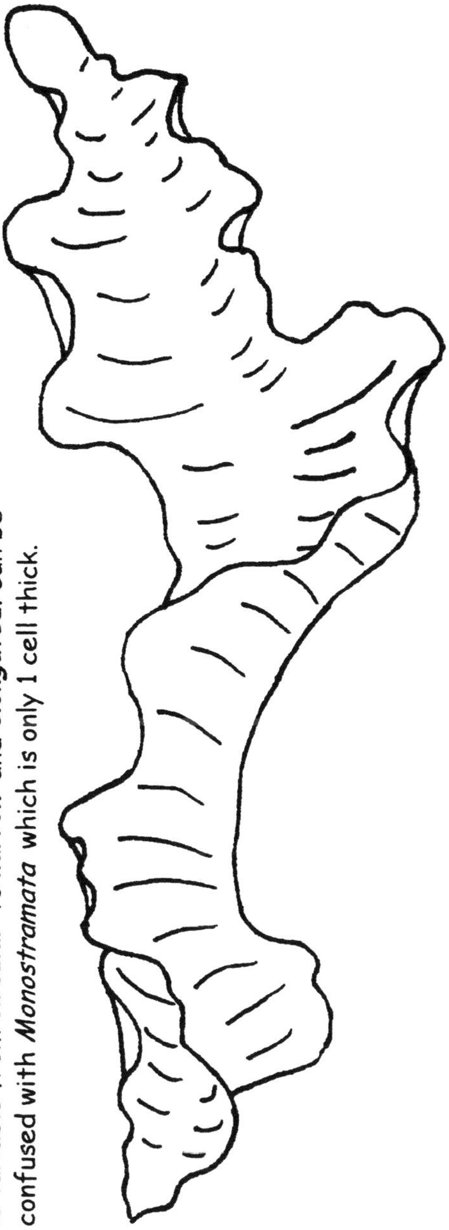

Sea Lettuce
(*Ulva lactuca*)
Edible. Bright green membranes only 2 cells thick. Shape is variable from ***circular*** to ***narrow*** and ***elongated***. Can be confused with *Monostramata* which is only 1 cell thick.

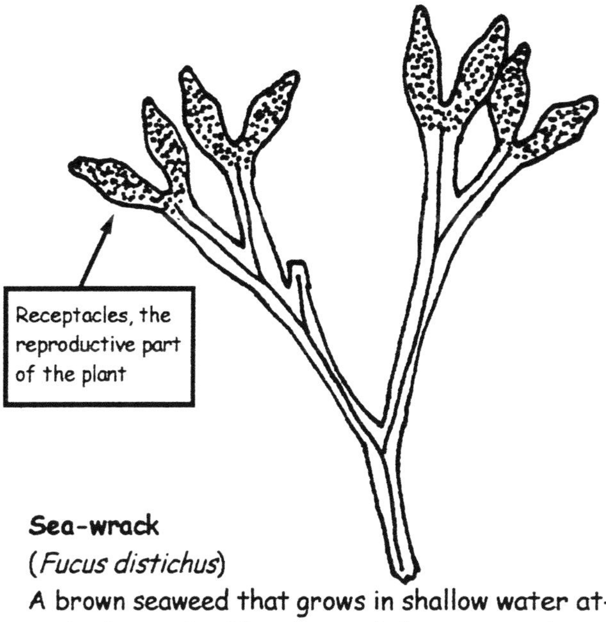

Sea-wrack
(*Fucus distichus*)
A brown seaweed that grows in shallow water attached to rocks. The shape of the receptacles of the fronds distinguishes it from other *Fucus* species. Pressed specimens will need to be taped or glued.

Sargasso Seaweed
(*Sargassum filipendula*)
Light brownish-green seaweed with air bladders on shorter braches. Very elaborate looking with "leaves" that have saw-toothed edges and a dis-tinct midrib.

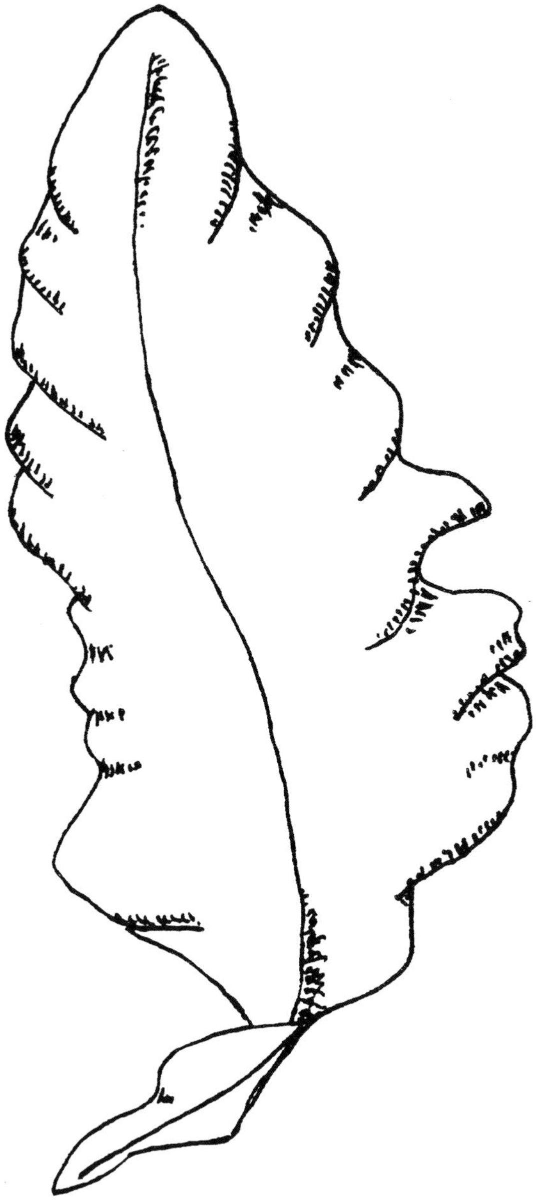

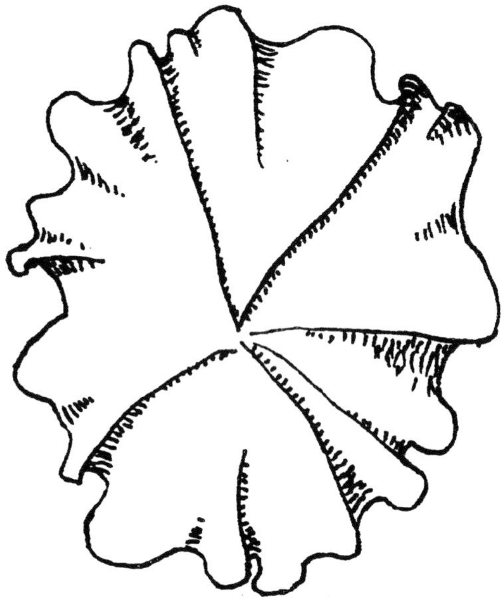

Nori, Purple Laver
(*Porphyra umbilicalis*)
Edible. Purple-brown or olive colored very thin membrane. May be more than 1 foot in diameter. Can be confused with *Ulva lactua* which is always bright green and also edible.

(*Grinnellia americana*)
Rose-red to pink 4-8 inches long with prominent mid-rib. Translucent membrane is only 1 cell thick. Attaches to wharves and rocks in quiet water. Can be confused with Porphyra which is darker and has no midrib.

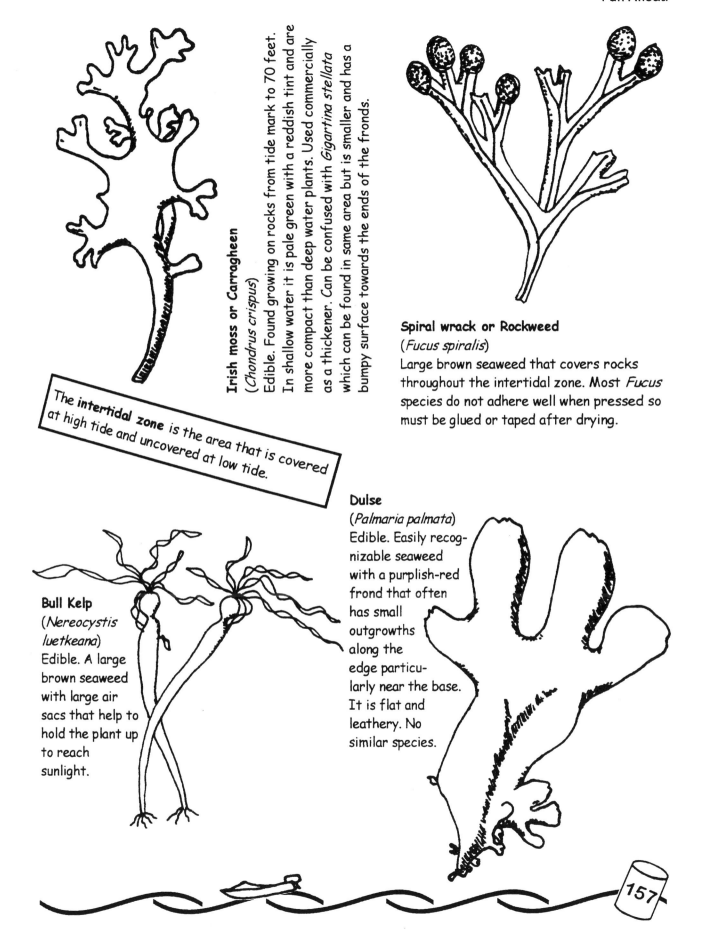

Irish moss or Carragheen
(*Chondrus crispus*)
Edible. Found growing on rocks from tide mark to 70 feet. In shallow water it is pale green with a reddish tint and are more compact than deep water plants. Used commercially as a thickener. Can be confused with *Gigartina stellata* which can be found in same area but is smaller and has a bumpy surface towards the ends of the fronds.

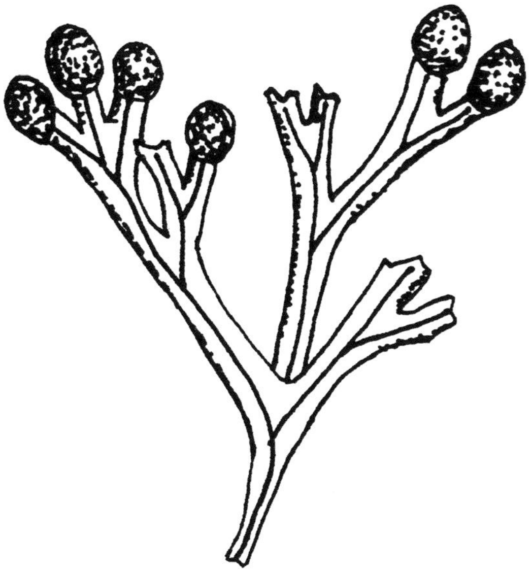

Spiral wrack or Rockweed
(*Fucus spiralis*)
Large brown seaweed that covers rocks throughout the intertidal zone. Most *Fucus* species do not adhere well when pressed so must be glued or taped after drying.

The **intertidal zone** is the area that is covered at high tide and uncovered at low tide.

Dulse
(*Palmaria palmata*)
Edible. Easily recognizable seaweed with a purplish-red frond that often has small outgrowths along the edge particularly near the base. It is flat and leathery. No similar species.

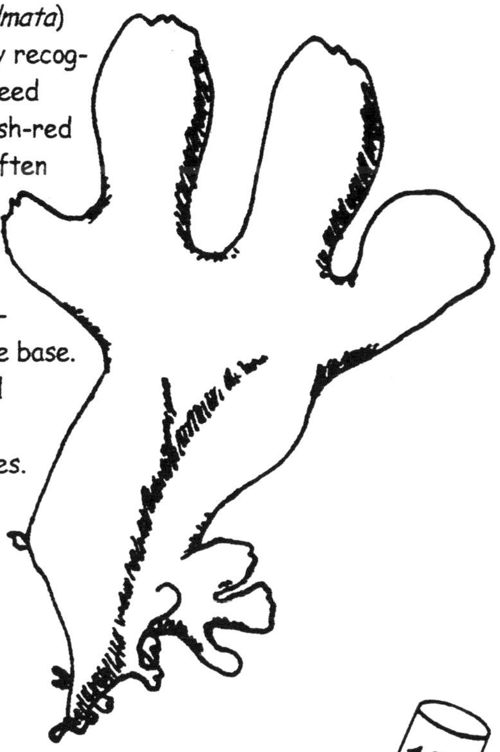

Bull Kelp
(*Nereocystis luetkeana*)
Edible. A large brown seaweed with large air sacs that help to hold the plant up to reach sunlight.

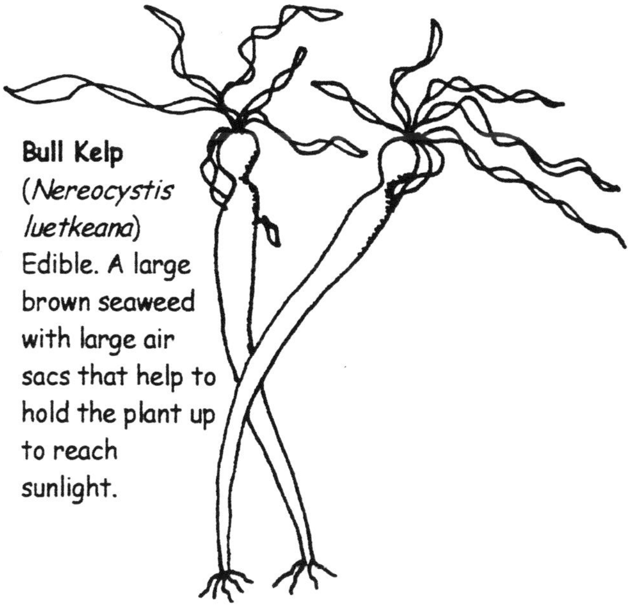

Some seaweeds have **receptacles** as part of their frond that are filled with a jelly like liquid. These are the reproductive parts of the plant.

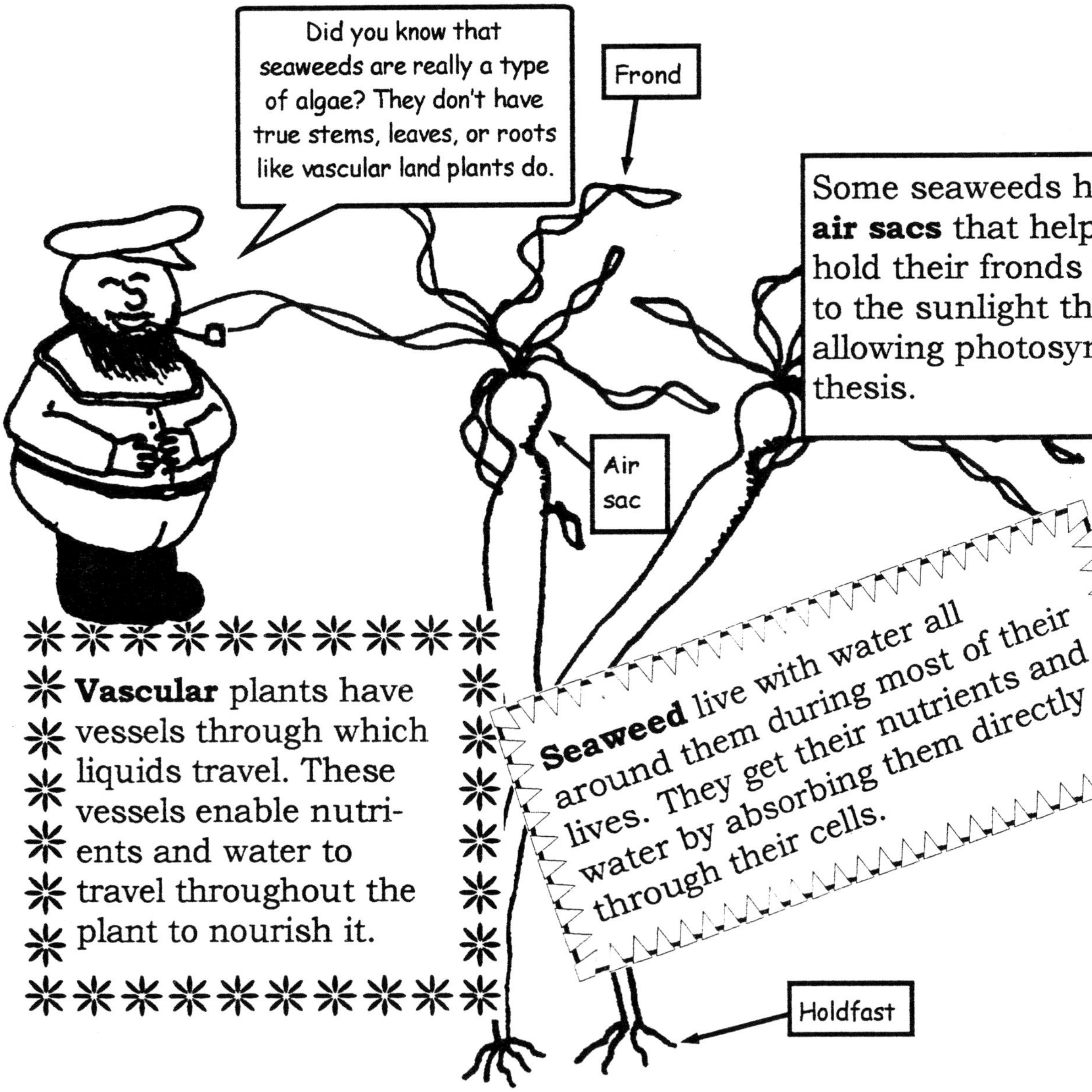

Did you know that seaweeds are really a type of algae? They don't have true stems, leaves, or roots like vascular land plants do.
Frond
Air sac
Holdfast

Some seaweeds have **air sacs** that help to hold their fronds up to the sunlight thus allowing photosynthesis.

Vascular plants have vessels through which liquids travel. These vessels enable nutrients and water to travel throughout the plant to nourish it.

Seaweed live with water all around them during most of their lives. They get their nutrients and water by absorbing them directly through their cells.

Seaweed have root-like structures called **holdfasts** whose only function is to hold onto rocks or other parts of the seafloor.

Plankton Identification Guide

*Plankton are **microscopic** (meaning able to be seen only with the aid of a microscope) and **macroscopic** (meaning able to be seen without the use of a microscope) plants and animals that drift with the winds and currents in marine and freshwater.*

Diatoms
microscopic

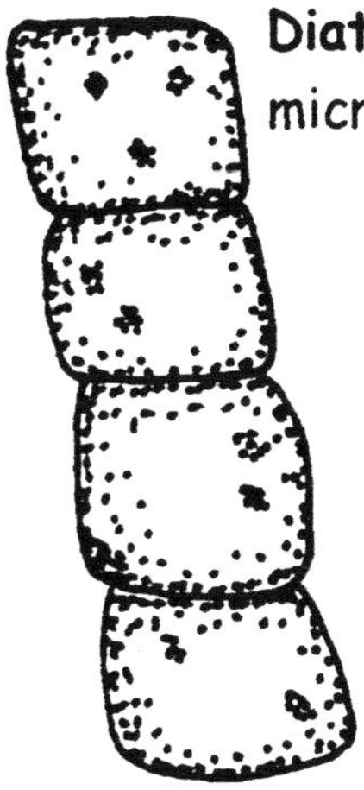

Dinoflagellates
microscopic

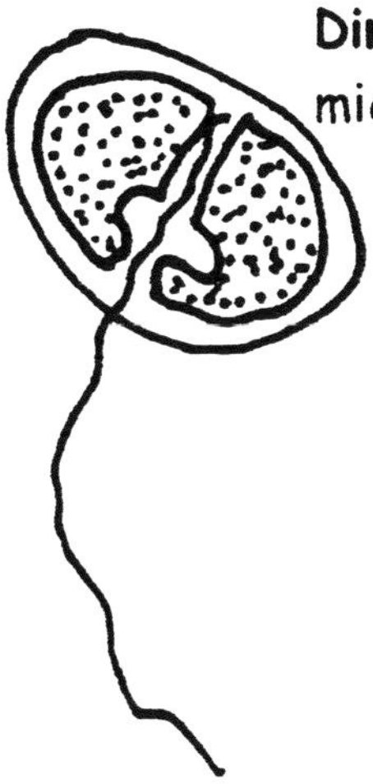

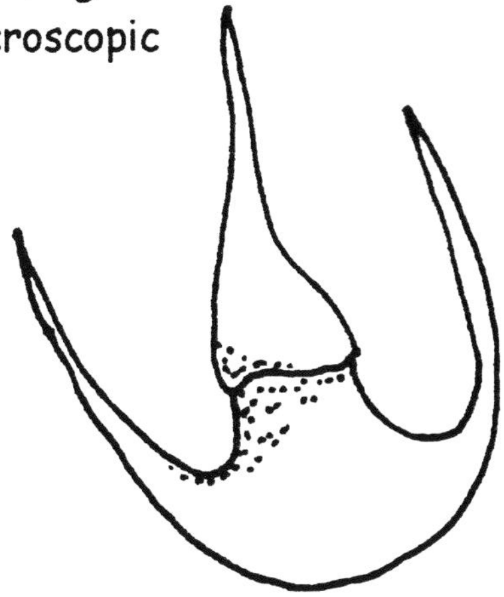

Phytoplankton live close to the surface of water to be near light so they may photosynthesize their food. They are usually unicellular. Some travel together in colonies.

Dinoflagellates resemble both plants and animals. They can propel themselves through the water yet photosynthesize their food. Some types create a chemical light called bioluminescence. Other kinds of dinoflagellates produce a strong neurotoxin and reproduce in mass “blooms,” called red-tides.

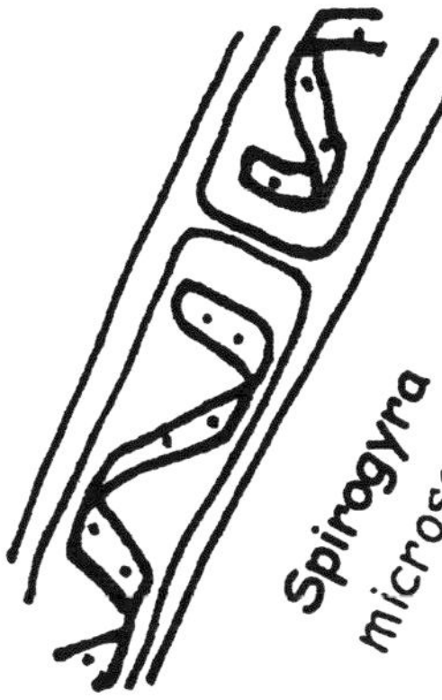

Spirogyra
microscopic

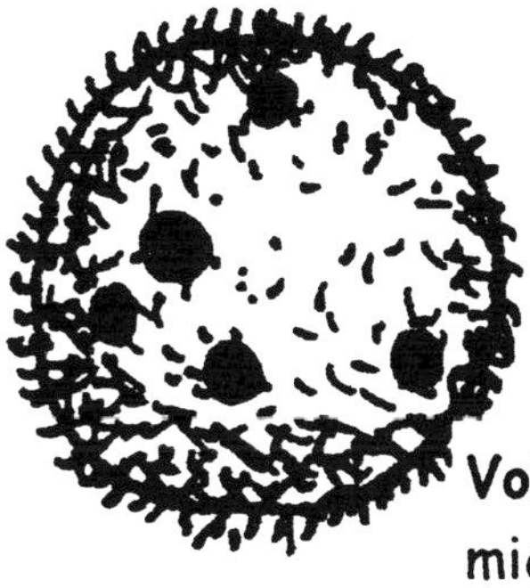

Volvox
microscopic

Zooplankton must capture other zooplankton or phytoplankton for food. There are several kinds, those that spend their whole lives as plankton (**holoplankton**) and those that spend part of their lives as plankton (**meroplankton**)

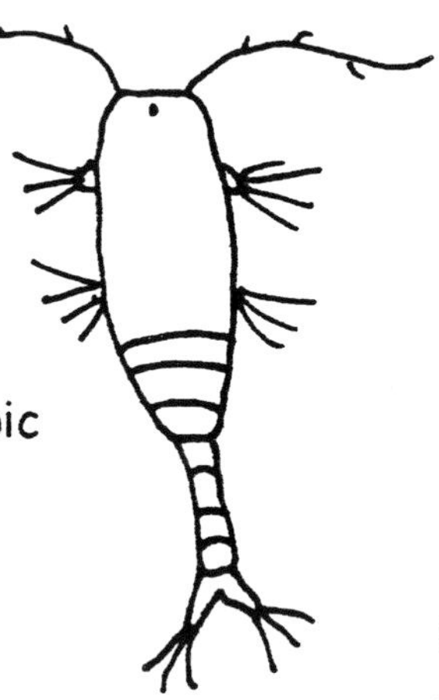

Copepod
macroscopic

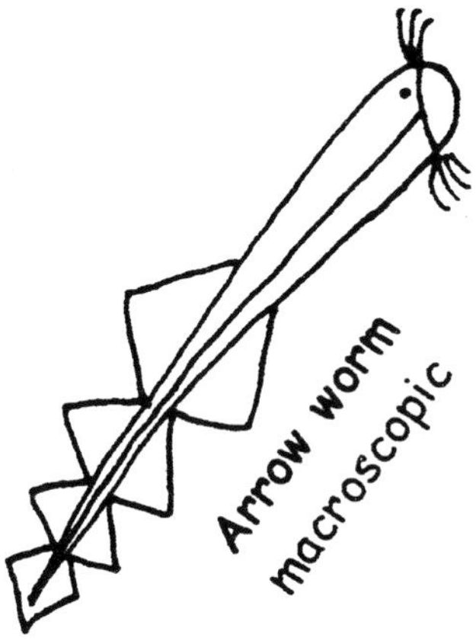

Arrow worm
macroscopic

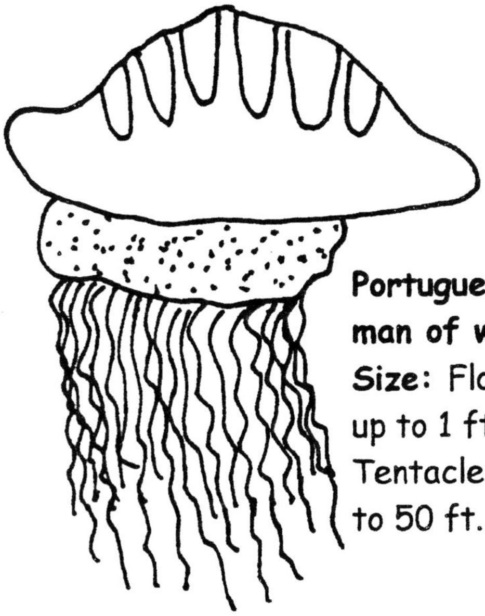

Portuguese man of war
Size: Float- up to 1 ft.
Tentacles-up to 50 ft.

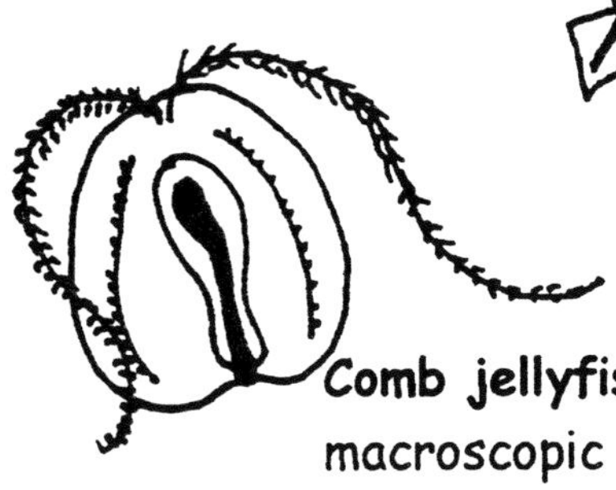

Comb jellyfish
macroscopic

Plankton include plants and animals both large and small that float in the water or are feeble swimmers that cannot propel themselves against waves and currents.

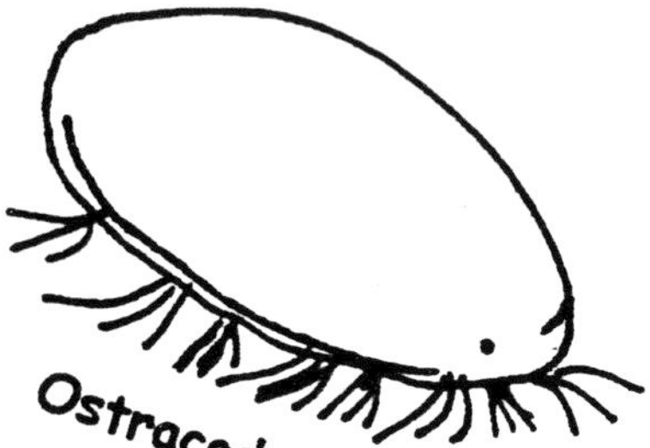

Ostracod
macroscopic

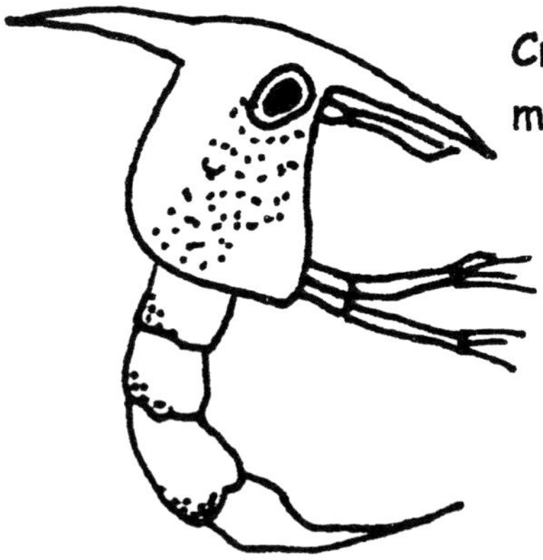

Crab Larvae
macroscopic

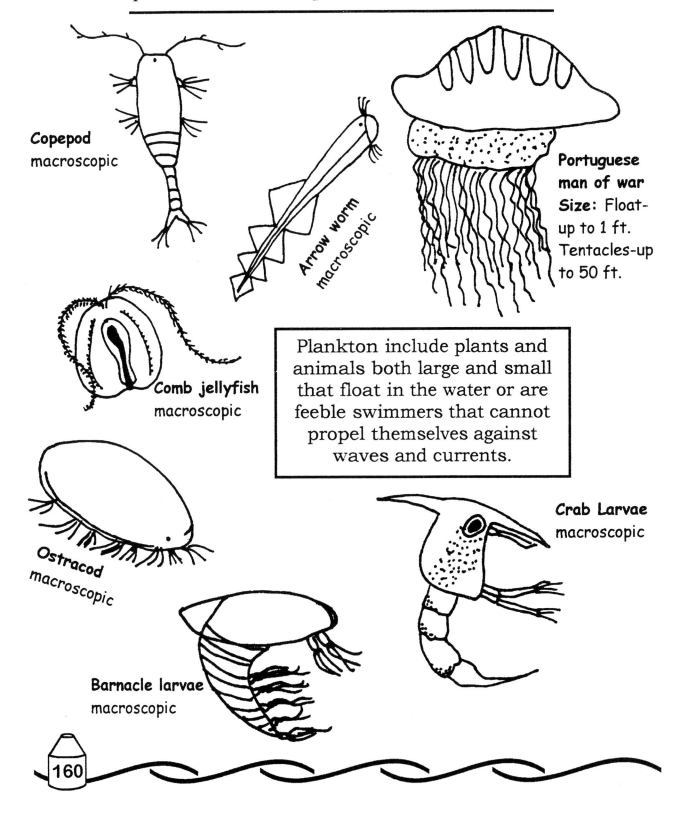

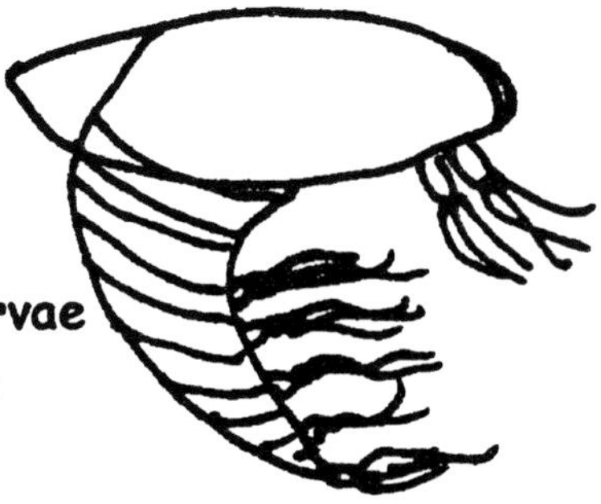

Barnacle larvae
macroscopic

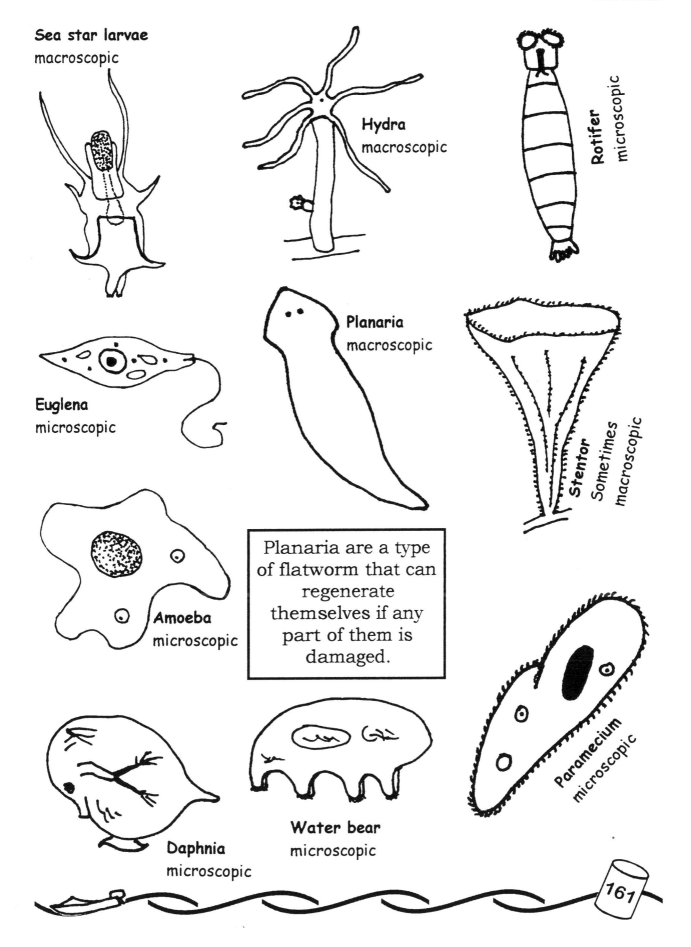

Sea star larvae
macroscopic

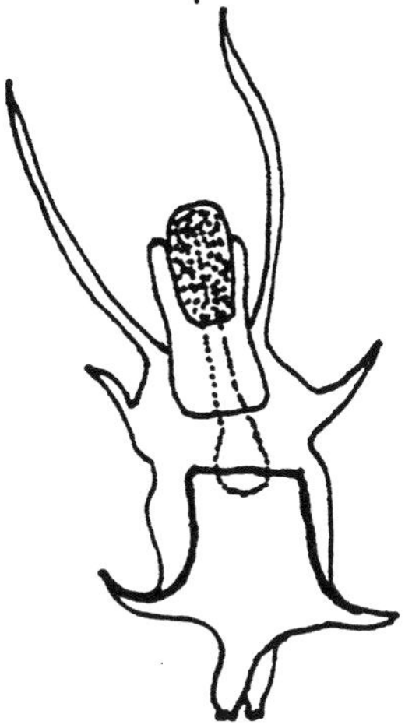

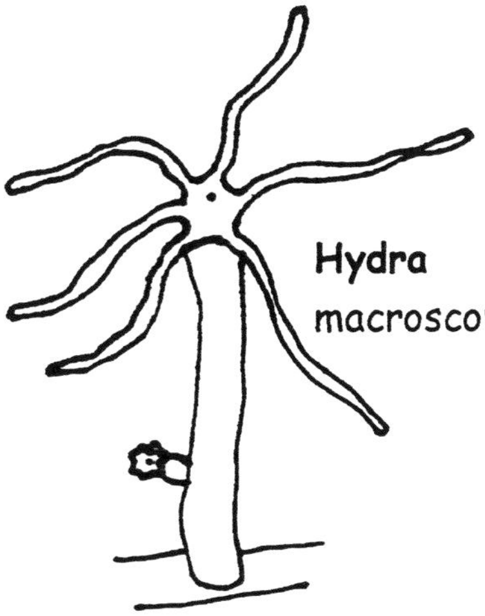

Hydra
macroscopic

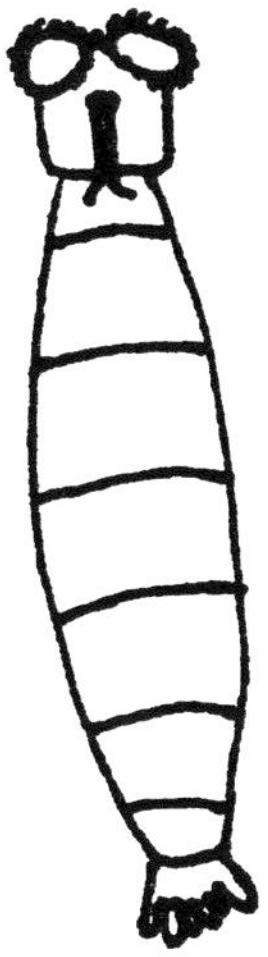

Rotifer
microscopic

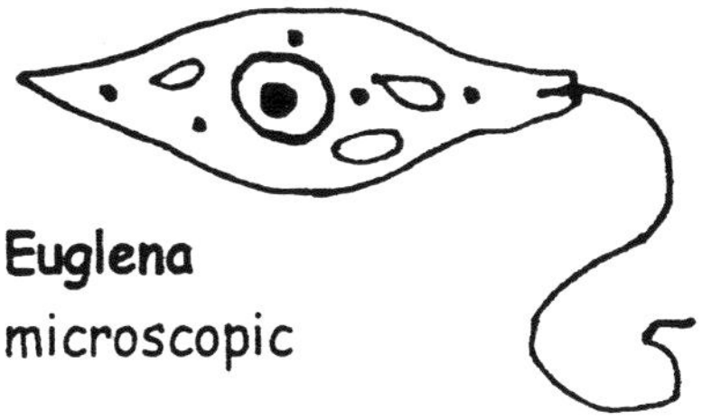

Euglena
microscopic

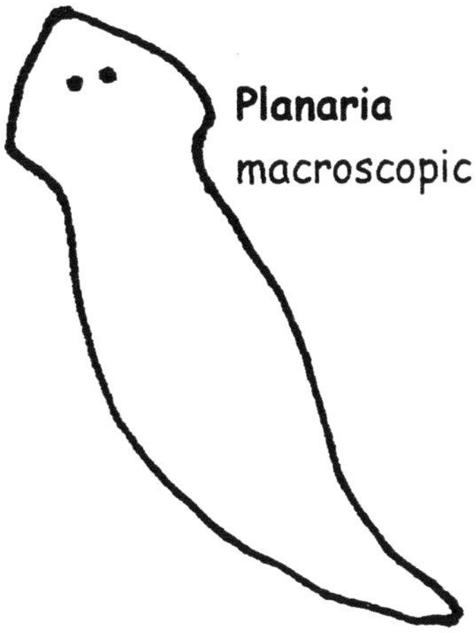

Planaria
macroscopic

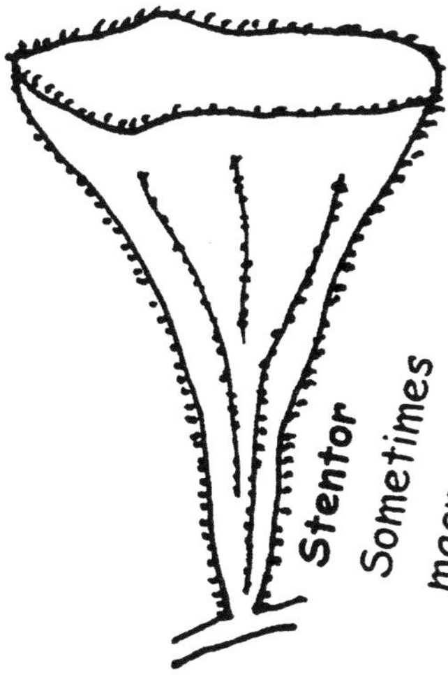

Stentor
Sometimes
macroscopic

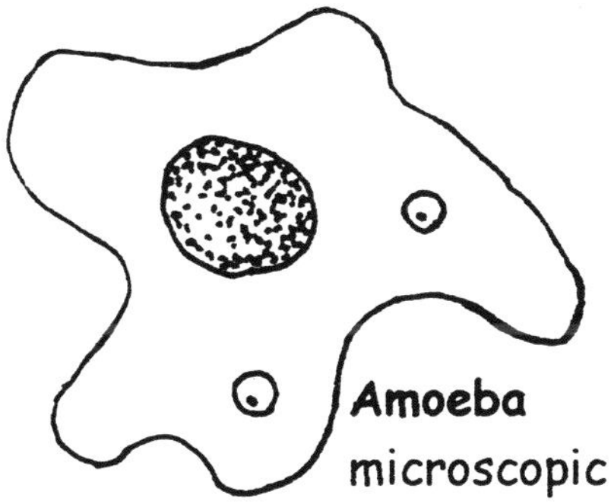

Amoeba
microscopic

Planaria are a type of flatworm that can regenerate themselves if any part of them is damaged.

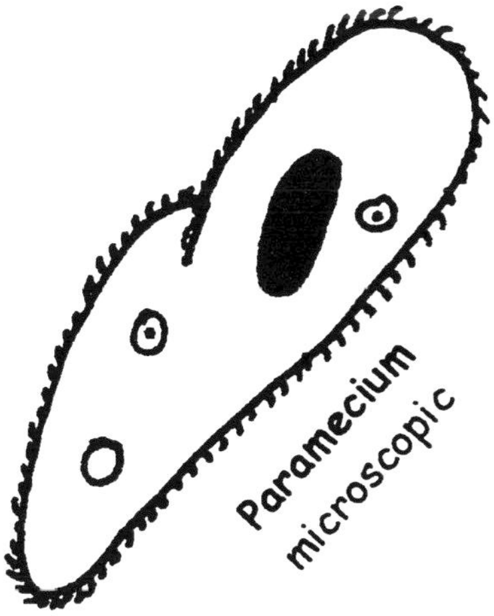

Paramecium
microscopic

Daphnia
microscopic

Water bear
microscopic

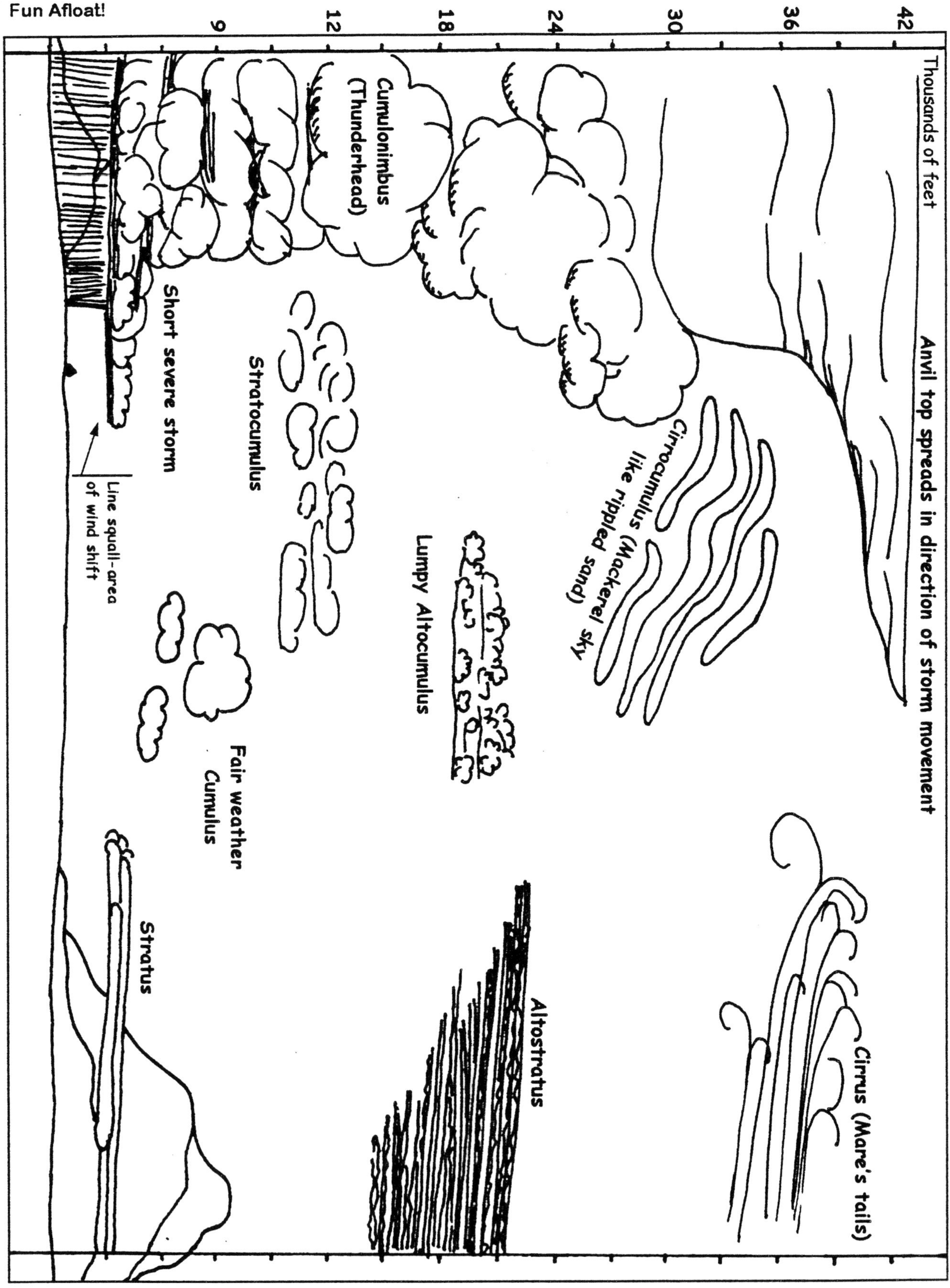
Thousands of feet
9
12
18
24
30
36
42
Anvil top spreads in direction of storm movement
Cumulonimbus (Thunderhead)
Cirrocumulus (Mackerel sky like rippled sand)
Short severe storm
Line squall-area of wind shift
Stratocumulus
Lumpy Altocumulus
Fair weather Cumulus
Stratus
Altostratus
Cirrus (Mare's tails)

The Bilge

Our little bilge rat, Earl

A

B

C

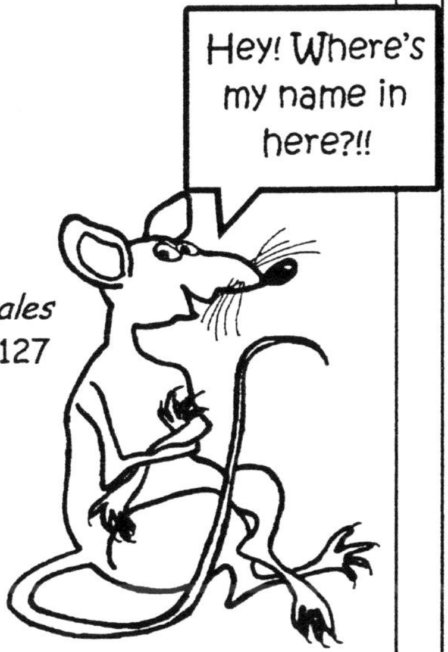
Hey! Where's my name in here?!!

D

E

F

G

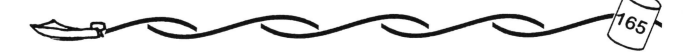

Sh! I'm sure they can't see me here!

O.K. so you found me on the last page but can you spot me on the next page? I'm not gonna say one word!

Bibliography

The Audubon Society. Field Guide to North American Fishes, Whales, and Dolphins. New York: Alfred A. Knopf, 1992.

Bleifeld, Maurice. Experimenting with a Microscope. New York: Venture, 1988.

Burch, David. Emergency Navigation. Camden, Maine: International Marine, 1990.

Carwardine, Mark; Hoyt, Eric; Fordyce, R. Ewan; and Gill, Peter. Whales, Dolphins, and Porpoises, The Nature Company Guide Series. San Francisco: Time-Life Books, 1998.

Corrigan, Patricia. The Whale Watcher's Guide. Minnetonka, Minnesota: Northword Press, 1999.

Coulombe, Deborah A. The Seaside Naturalist. New York: Simon and Schuster, 1992.

Encarta Encyclopedia 2000 on CD-ROM. USA: Microsoft Corporation, 1999.

Eyges, Leonard. The Practical Pilot. Camden, Maine: International Marine, 1990.

Gill, Peter. Whales Dolphins & Porpoises, The Little Guides Series. San Francisco: Fog City Press, 2000.

Gross, M. Grant. Oceanography: A View of the Earth, 5th Edition. Englewood Cliffs, NJ: Prentice Hall, 1990.

Johnson, Gaylord and Bleifield, Maurice. Hunting with the Microscope. New York: Prentice Hall Press, 1987.

Leatherwood, Stephen and Reeves, Randall R. The Sierra Club Handbook of Whales and Dolphins. San Francisco: Sierra Club Books, 1983.

Lee, Thomas F. The Seaweed Handbook. New York: Dover Publications, Inc., 1986.

Maloney, Elbert S. Chapman Piloting: Seamanship and Small Boat Handling, 62nd Edition. New York: International Marine, 1990.

National Geographic Society. Exploring your World: The Adventure of Geography. Washington, D.C.: National Geographic Society, 1993.

Schaefer, Vincent J. and Day, John A. A Field Guide to the Atmosphere. The Peterson Field Guide Series. Boston: Houghton Mifflin Co., 1981.

Simon, Seymour. How to be an Ocean Scientist in your Own Home. New York: J. B. Lippincott, 1988.

Villiard, Paul. The Hidden World: The Story of Microscopic Life. New York: Four Winds Press, 1975.

World Book Encyclopedia Millennium 2000 Edition on CD-ROM, Version 4.0. USA: World Book Inc., 1999.

Resource List

Books about the Ocean and Ocean Life

The Ocean Book: Aquarium and Seaside Activities for All Ages. Center for Marine Conservation. John Wiley and Sons. Somerset, NY. Grades Pre-K-5.

Projects in Oceanography. Simon, S. (Science at Work Series). Franklin Watts. Chicago, IL.

The Marine Biology Coloring Book. Nielson, Thomas. Harper Collins. Scranton, PA. Grades 7-12.

The Oceans. Bramwell, Martyn. 1987 Franklin Watts.

Beachcraft Bonanza. Heinz, Brian. 1985 Ballyhoo Books. Shoreham, NY.

Marine Mammals of the World. FAO Species Identification Guide. T.A. Jefferson, S. Leatherwood, and M.A. Weber. 1993. FAO, Rome. Also available in CD-ROM form.

Marine Mammals and Sea Turtles of the U.S. Atlantic and Gulf of Mexico. K. Wynne and M. Schwartz. 1999. Rhode Island Sea Grant, RI.

Resources available from WhaleNet

Marine Science Activities on a Budget: a booklet that contains oceanographic activities that can be tailored to different grade levels.

The World of Whales, Dolphins, and Porpoises-Interdisciplinary Curriculum Units for Pre-K through High School: a book that contains more than 200 pages of activities that are interdisciplinary and suitable for differing abilities, and interests.

Marine Science Bibliography: a pamphlet with an extensive list of references for a wide range of grade levels, interests, and disciplines.

Contact Person and Address for Ordering:

J. Michael Williamson of WhaleNet
MICS
20 Moynihan Rd.
So. Hamilton, MA 01982

Order online at the web address below:

http://whale.wheelock.edu

Other Resources

Edmund Scientific Co.
101 East Gloucester Pike
Barrington, NJ 08007
Tel. # 609-547-3488
Tel. # 1-800-728-6999
FAX 609-573-6840
http://www.edsci.com
Sell material for science projects and items related to astronomy, biology, anatomy, zoology, light, lasers, more. Also sellers of field microscopes.

Center for Marine Conservation
National Office
1725 DeSales St. NW
Washington, D.C. 20036
Tel. # 202-429-5609
http://www.cmc-ocean.org/
This organization has monitoring and international beach clean-up programs where volunteers are needed. They also sell marine curriculum involving pollution and how to save our seas. International Coastal Clean-up telephone # : 1-800-CMC-BEACH (U.S. only) or 757-851-6734.

Skycraft
Parts & Surplus, Inc.
Featuring electronics and other government surplus.
http://www.Skycraftsurplus.com

So Long! Hope you had fun! Like my grandpappy, Billy Bilge Rat, always used to say...Keep the wet stuff on the outside of the boat!

Order Books from Fortworks Publishing	Qty.	Cost	Total
Fun Afloat! Cool Activities for Families that Boat 170 pgs.		$19.95	
Flag Journal 52 pgs.		$2.95	
Weather Tracking Journal 52 pgs.		$2.95	
Fishing Log 52 pgs.		$2.95	
Marina/Anchorage Journal 100 pgs.		$4.95	
Marine Animal Tracking Journal 52 pgs.		$2.95	
Boat Journal 52 pgs.		$2.95	
Customized Ship's Log 100 pgs. Send us your boat's name and a photo for the weather proof laminated cover.		$9.95	
Florida Scavenger Hunt 28 pgs.		$1.50	
		Subtotal:	
Florida Residents add 6% Sales Tax			
Shipping and handling:		$0-$6.00 add $1.75 $6.01-$20.00 add $3.00 Over $20.00 add 15%	
		Total:	
Send check or money order in U.S. Funds only to:		**Fortworks Publishing P.O. Box 6766 Titusville, FL 32782-6766**	
Visa/Mastercard #:		Expiration Date:	
Name:		Phone #:	
Address to ship:		City:	
State/ Province:		Postal Code:	

All of our books are fully guaranteed. If you are unhappy with a book for any reason, just return it to us within 30 days for a full refund.

Visit our website for more information about books available from

Fortworks Publishing

http://publishing.fortworks.com

E-mail us: publishing@fortworks.com

Other Books available from Fortworks Publishing!

LOOK!

<u>Florida Scavenger Hunt</u>: Do you live in Florida? Or, are you planning a trip? Go on a Florida scavenger hunt with this booklet. Families can play together as one team or group into multiple teams for a light-hearted competition. Individuals can have fun searching on their own. Schools and organizations can form teams for a fun competition. This booklet contains a 20 item hunt list with room to glue, staple, or tape each item as it is found. Each team needs a hunt booklet. 28 pages. $5\frac{1}{2}$"x$8\frac{1}{2}$" $1.50

Comb Bound Journals for Journal Activities in Fun Afloat!

Order these inexpensive comb bound journals ready for your information without the need to photocopy anything.

Boat Journal: 52 journal pages with enough room to document over 100 boats. Room to record boat name, address, e-mail, crew names, home port, a comments section and more. Staple boat cards to the journal page edges! Comb bound. $8\frac{1}{2}$"x11" **$2.95**

Anchorage/Marina Journal: 100 journal pages with room to document 50 anchorages and 100 marinas. The anchorage pages have room for a photo or drawing of each anchorage and a large area for comments. On the marina pages you can document information about approaching and contacting, proximity to shopping and restaurants, weather protection, and much more. Comb bound. $8\frac{1}{2}$"x11" **$4.95**

Marine Animal Tracking Journal: 52 journal pages including room to record over 300 animal sightings with areas for position, behavior, number, time and date. Plus, we've added journal pages to record 40 in-depth animal sightings with room for photos or drawings and areas for weather, water density and visibility, and a large area to record behavior. Comb bound. $8\frac{1}{2}$"x11" **$2.95**

Customized Ship's Log: Send us a color photo of your boat along with its name and type, and we'll create a custom ship's log with a full color picture of your boat on the weather-proof laminated cover. 100 journal pages with room to record time, helmsman, compass heading, average speed, distance traveled, % cloud cover, sea state, wind direction and speed, and barometric pressure. Plus there's a large area to write comments. Each page has room for 12 entries and can cover 1 full day of a passage if recorded every 2 hours or 2 full days of a passage if recorded every 4 hours. Comb bound. $8\frac{1}{2}$"x11" **$9.95**

Weather Tracking Journal: 52 journal pages. On each journal page you can record a week's worth of weather information recording it twice a day. That means you can record a full year of weather in this journal! Areas for time, temperature, barometric pressure, cloud type and cover, visibility, wind strength and direction, rainfall, and wave height. Comb bound. 11"x$8\frac{1}{2}$" **$2.95**

Flag Journal: 52 journal pages. Document 52 country's flags and the ships you see flying them. Includes a large area for a drawing of each country's flag plus space to write in information you learn about each country. Comb bound. $8\frac{1}{2}$"x11" **$2.95**

Fishing Log: 52 journal pages with space to document over 200 fishing excursions. Record information about baits/lures used, fishing location, weather, sea state, fish caught, and more. Comb bound. $8\frac{1}{2}$"x11" **$2.95**